Rock 'n Roll Customer Service

Jeff Nash

Because "I still haven't found what I'm looking for"
U2

Rock 'n Roll Customer Service

Copyright © 2009 Jeff Nash

All rights reserved, including the right to reproduce this book or portions thereof in any form whatsoever without express written permission of the author.

Printed in the United States of America

17 16 15 14 13 12 11 10 09   1 2 3 4 5

First Edition

ISBN: 1441436022
EAN-13: 9781441436023

Contents

5	Foreword by Tom DeLapp
7	Prologue: Are You Ready To Rock 'n Roll?
11	Pop Quiz
17	Who Are You?
23	Show Time…Five Customer Needs
29	Pet Peeves
33	"No Soup For You!" (Bad Service)
41	Common Shortfalls
51	Rock Star Status (Good Service)
59	Three Genres of Service
63	Face-to-Face
69	Telephone
81	E-mail
89	Stalkers & Critics: Difficult Customers
97	My World Tour: The Welcome Center
105	Customer Service Revival
117	Secret to Great Service

Foreword

By Tom DeLapp, President
Communication Resources for Schools

When you interviewed for your job, did you ever think of it as an audition? Maybe you should have. I'm a big believer in the performing arts. When you're on stage in a live performance there are no gimmicks, no edits or second takes, and no do-overs. You're judged every time by your audience on that one performance. You also have a direct and personal relationship with the crowd. How well you perform decides whether you are a flop, a one-hit wonder, or a star. Actors, dancers, singers and musicians are some of the most courageous people I know because they put themselves and their production on the line every time they step on stage.

In my 35 years in educational "show" business, working with over 400 school districts, I've come to this conclusion: customer service in education is a performing art and your schools are the stage. In a very real sense, public education is a live performance . . . just like a rock concert. When we attend concerts, whether they're in large arenas or intimate coffee houses, we want the same things as customers. We want value for our investment of time, money and involvement. We want to come away with a lasting positive impression. We want to be engaged in the shared experience and to even sing along and participate. We want satisfaction, but sometimes, in the words of Mick Jagger, We "can't get no satisfaction." We also want to feel like the people on stage are performing just for us. The goal for the performer is that the customer walks away with a smile on his or her face, humming a memorable little ditty that sticks in their mind, and that they rave about to their friends. Isn't that what we want from our customers in the public schools? A great experience! Raving fans!

Jeff Nash gets it. In *Rock 'n Roll Customer Service* he gives us new insights into an old problem – building strong customer relationships. He sees that we aren't there just to do our jobs, but to *perform* our jobs and be part of an award-winning production. Whether we are the "sage on the stage" teaching in a classroom or behind the scenes making the system run smoothly, we are all on a public stage. Our rock concert tour is a series of one-night stands that spans about 185 school days a year. Each day is a new chance to perform for our diverse audiences. Each of us needs to know our part, deliver our lines, hit the right notes, and choreograph our steps for the performance to succeed. We each are soloists when we interact with our customers, but collectively we all make or break the production.

Your job in public schools isn't about implementing lesson plans, managing spreadsheets, handling work orders, cleaning buildings, answering phones, driving buses, or filing compliance reports; it's about people and how well we meet their expectations as we perform these tasks. We are a "people" business and the relationships we maintain with our internal and external customers are the key.

The funny thing is that we now have a mixed generation of parents and employees. But all of these Baby Boomer, Gen X, and Millennial grandparents, parents and colleagues have one thing in common . . . we all share the same music in our lives. There's a popular TV show on the air now called, "Don't Forget the Lyrics." The premise is that we all can remember lyrics and messages delivered to memorable tunes over the last fifty years. If you hacked into our iPods or thumbed through our shelves of CDs or record albums you would find an eclectic collection of musical genres from oldies to pop; rap to reggae. But the one thing connecting all of these generations is good old-fashioned Rock 'n Roll.

Unfortunately, with the pressures of the job, many of us have become tone deaf. We aren't really aware of how we come across. We all think we're the ones delivering excellent service; it's just the others who aren't. But that's like singing in the shower and expecting to be the next American Idol. As you read through this book, you can benefit from Jeff's "vocal coaching" to see if your style and delivery is on key and rocking the house. The performance of our schools depends on the seamless orchestration of every performer and this book can get your team on the same song sheet singing in harmony.

When you look at some of the most enduring rock groups, they succeed because they have a reputation for quality and consistency. They deliver the goods time and again. Is your school, department, or district like that? Whether you're a newbie, a mid-career burnout, or a set-in-your-ways old timer, it's time to get in touch with your inner rock star. Rock 'n Roll doesn't have to mean being caught between a rock and a hard place or rolling with the punches from your customers. Become a part of a customer service revival in your district by believing in yourself, your colleagues and your organization. The spotlight is on you and it's time to be an education rock star. It's your legacy, and your job!

Prologue: Are You Ready To Rock 'n Roll?

Dim the house lights, turn up the stage lights and crank up the fog machine. The show is about to begin. Sure, you may not know all the lyrics, but rock with us as we go on a customer service world tour.

Who would have thunk it? Someone actually had the misguided notion of combining two things as unintroduced (which my computer says is not a real word – though it should be and you can feel free to use it as such) as **Rock 'n Roll** and **customer service** – and he even had the audacity to write a book about it. How do these things fit together? Or do they relate at all?

Well, after working to author a book about customer service on and off for a couple years, I decided to get some professional help, but not necessarily the help you are rightfully thinking I need. No, the help I got came from a woman I have known for years as a friend, a neighbor and a proofreader. That's right, I asked Sharon to help me finally get this book out of my head and onto paper. I thought she would laugh me out of the room when I told her the book was designed to use Rock 'n Roll lyrics as a foundation for provoking a customer service paradigm shift among school personnel. To my surprise, she didn't laugh at all. In fact, her direct quote was, "Rock 'n Roll without music is simply poetry!"

Wow! What do you say to that? I wasn't even sure we were in the same conversation! Anyway, Sharon's response did nothing to convince me she knew where I was coming from, but it did tell me she had an open mind to the concept I would soon explain to her. And I hope you will have an open mind as well.

This book is designed to challenge you to examine your own attitude toward customer service. What kind of rocker are you? Hard? Progressive? Classic? Punk? Does your rock style mirror your approach to customer service? We will discuss plenty of tips and suggestions along the way, but none of that matters if the mindset is out of whack. It is important for you to use this book as a mirror. I want you to frequently measure your customer service attitude and habits against the things you will read – the examples, the stories and the how-to's – kind of like a band might monitor the Billboard chart. And congrats! The fact you have read this far suggests you are seeking improvement in your own performance. Great! Too many school system employees give the appearance of overconfidence in their own abilities. Complacency is king in some school districts. I don't want you to be a one hit wonder.

Rock 'n Roll is helping us frame the discussion. Look closely, and you may see some serious wisdom in the lyrics – or, according to Sharon, the poetry. Songwriters often have a story to share. Others have a message to convey or even a warning to deliver.

The following chapters are written in a nutty manner. Trust me, it is done on purpose. I tried to incorporate a conversational style. If ever you find this book stuffy or boring, please put it down and find something better to do with your time. However, if you find it entertaining while informative, then give it to a friend – nope, check that, encourage a friend to purchase his own copy! Also, drop me a line after you have completed it. I would welcome your feedback as well as your own customer service stories and suggestions.

And now…(drum roll please)…we're going to go "behind the music", so to speak, and uncover the untold stories, dirty little secrets and phenomenal success stories of school customer service. We will focus an unblinking eye on those things we, in everyday life, prefer not to notice, see and acknowledge.

Step inside! Hello!
We've the most amazing show
You'll enjoy it all we know
Step inside! Step inside!
<u>Karn Evil 9</u> - Emerson, Lake and Palmer

Pop Quiz

Don't worry your mind
When you give it your best
One, two, one, two – this is just a test!

Just a Test - Beastie Boys

What do you mean, pop quiz? Rock 'n Roll is about getting out on stage and jamming, not about taking tests. But consider it this way, before the song can be released, we have to try it out at a few local venues just to test the waters. Think of it as an impromptu gig. So tune up your guitars, er, I mean brains, and let's rock.

Now, go ahead and find something with which to write. Got it? Great. Next, I want you to answer the following two questions with complete honesty. **It is important that you write your answers and not just think about them** (use a napkin if you want to feel like a real old school songwriter). The impact will be greater when you can see the answers in front of you. And we will continue to reference them as we proceed through the following chapters. Feel free to write the answers inside the front cover of this book – in ink you Rock 'n Roll rebel! More importantly, be sure not to overanalyze your responses. Like listening to a new album for the first time, simply write down the first answer that comes to mind.

Are you ready? Here goes.

Question 1: What percentage of employees in your district do not offer good customer service consistently?

Be sure to consider all district employees. Factor in your individual school personnel, bus drivers, administrative office staff, payroll department, technology services, child nutrition employees, custodians, substitute teachers, and so on.

Have you written your answer yet? If not, you are thinking too much.

The good news is there can be no right or wrong answers on this two-question quiz. Unlike some American Idols, you cannot fail. The bad news is the first question is not a fair question. However, neither is it a "gotcha". I realize you may want to complain about the first question. After all, I love to use this question to open up my customer service training sessions, and I have heard all the complaints. Yeah, yeah, yeah – I know it contains two variables that we have yet to define. Get over it.

Did you recognize the variables? We have not defined "good customer service" and thus it becomes an unfair question. Neither have we discussed the concept of "consistently". Of course, our own perspectives of these notions correlate directly to our answers. But, hey, Rock 'n Roll is a personal thing! Let's move on to the next question.

Question 2: Do *YOU* offer good customer service consistently?

What? A little too close for comfort? Well as Dr. Phil says, "We can't change what we don't acknowledge." You may also notice that the variables still impact this answer but at least they are consistent with our own perceptions as applied to the answer we wrote for the first question.

Let's consider the first question. **What percentage of employees in your district do not offer good customer service consistently?** In a concert hall full of screaming fans, or a training room full of educators, there are a variety of answers in a remarkably wide range. Even still, I love this question because it helps create a foundation for continued discussion.

Now, I may not own a grammy, but after issuing this quiz at countless training sessions, I started noticing a trend. You see, one of my favorite activities is to have participants call out the numbers they wrote in response to the first question, and we record them. Next, we figure out the average.

I observed, even with the wide ranges offered by each class, the average *always* seemed to fall between 37% and 43%. In an effort to be witty, I created a little card with "37% - 43%" written on it. In training sessions, I would wait for the volunteer to tell me the average calculated, and then I would hold up my card for everyone to see. They were quite impressed!

Keep in mind this training was always conducted within my own school district. With 17,000 employees, there are plenty of guinea pigs, er, I mean participants. After many sessions with similar averages, I deduced, within my district, roughly 40% (or 7,200) of the employees do not offer good customer service consistently.

Once I started my road trips, traveling the state and the nation training other school personnel, I was startled to find the 37-43 rule applicable everywhere. Here, I thought it was just my district. Instead, though enlightened, I was at the same time both distraught and relieved to find such large numbers of school personnel nationwide were suffering the same struggles. I was distraught to think children and families everywhere are victims of poor service, but relieved that my district is not the only one facing this struggle.

The first time I gave this quiz outside of my own district I was conducting a training session for the North Carolina School Public Relations Association. The group included public information officers from many of the school districts around the state. I had no idea what number they would offer in response to the first question. Each district is unique, and there is no way to find value in their class average. But I still had my little "37% - 43%" card ready to share.

We took the quiz, averaged the answers, and wouldn't you know it? The class average was exactly 40%! I held up my pre-made card, and they thought I was a genius. It was truly an "a-ha" moment for all of us. Since that day, I have given this quiz in many different states to many different collections of attendees and found the 37-43 rule still holds true.

Obviously, I don't know what number you wrote down, but I will presumptuously assume that if we could somehow average the scores of our readers, it would register exactly 40% (he says with a wink). Hence, let's use the 40% number to frame our discussion. True, the aforementioned variables dilute its muscle, but the fact that this figure surfaces time and again makes it, at least in my mind, a statistic on which we can hang our collective guitars.

I would hope you are beginning to develop a sense of outrage – sort of like Woodstock (right on, man). You should be forming some questions in your mind as you continue reading. First of all, ask yourself: Is 40% a satisfactory number? Are you pleased with the notion that 40% of the people wearing the badge for your school district are not offering good service consistently? I would certainly hope not. Not only should that number disappoint you, it should DISGUST you. I want you to be passionately infuriated by this finding. So what would be an acceptable number? I hesitate any time I throw that question to the crowd for fear of a Jerry Springer episode breaking out. Inevitably, someone will shout out, "Zero. Our goal should be zero percent." Then somebody else will counter with, "That's not realistic." Soon thereafter, all you-know-what breaks loose. Like the Blues Brothers, we will have a *"Riot in Cell Block Number Nine."*

In what sounds like an attempt to avoid answering my own question, the acceptable number sought in the above paragraph must be decided locally. Yeah, I know. That sounds like lip-syching – a total copout (no offense to Milli Vanilli).

The next logical questions are: How did this happen? And, Can we afford to do nothing and hope it gets better? If we stick our heads in the sand and come back together a year from now, will our number be any better? No! Of course not. It will only get worse if we don't interject great efforts to improve it. In Rock 'n Roll you're only as good as your next big hit. What have you done for me lately?

Think back to your first job interview with the school district. You were probably asked that silly question that we all get asked (and likely still ask when we are the interviewers): Why do you want this job?

Well, duh! Nobody ever says they want it for the money. After all, educators know the score when it comes to underfunded salaries. And regardless of the real reasons, job candidates typically come up with some fairly noble answers. They might say, "I want to positively impact the lives of children," or maybe, "I have a need to give back to my community," or some other mushy response. Yes, they can get quite artsy in their answers, but I still believe we are wired with the desire to actually accomplish those ideals. Nobody ever said at an interview (with hands on hips) "I want to see how many people I can tick off in one day!"

I believe we all want to help people. We really mean those flowery answers. In fact, I'll bet on the first day of our new school system jobs, we all got up early, showered and put on our best outfits. We were careful to make sure our hair was just right, and we arrived early with great intentions. But somehow, 40% of us spiraled downward from those good intentions on the first day to a place where we now fail to offer good service consistently. How did this occur? If we cannot figure out the cause, we cannot prescribe a cure. Our chapter about bad service will talk more about the reasons. Be sure to have your highlighter handy.

Let's move on to the ever-important second question. Do *YOU* offer good customer service consistently? OK, by a show of hands how many of you answered "Yes" for the second question? How many indicated you *DO* offer good service consistently? Usually, nearly every hand goes up. We typically see nearly 100% of the participants telling us their own service is consistently good while that of 40% of their co-workers is not. Guess what readers, 40% of you are lying!

Can truth come out of lying?
<u>Happy When I'm Crying</u> – Pearl Jam

I have pondered this contradiction for years. Why does everyone erroneously think their own level of service is good, but can easily spot the faults of those around them?

Only recently have I reached a conclusion. I would hypothesize that we too often relate being a good customer service representative to being a good person. Yes, being a good person is likely a great foundation for becoming a good customer service representative, but in no way does there exist a direct one-to-one correlation. Heck, even Gandhi, one of the dearest gentleman to walk the planet, may have been a horrible customer service representative for all we know. My point is there is more to it than just being nice. However, since we like to think of ourselves as nice people, we automatically transfer that self-approval to our own customer service habits. I believe this is a major contributor to the breakdown that leads to numbers hovering around 40%. In the coming chapters, we will discuss ways to become ***good*** customer service representatives. At the very end of the book, I will share my thoughts on customer service ***great***ness.

Thanks for being a good sport and taking the quiz. I hope it has brought attention to the widespread need for customer service improvement. Keep the 40% number in mind as we proceed.

You see I lied myself before
And I think I know the score
<u>You Can't Lie To A Liar</u> – Dan McCafferty

"Who Are You?"

Well, who are you? (Who are you? Who, who, who, who?)
I really wanna know (Who are you? Who, who, who, who?)

Who Are You? – The Who

The Who asks a rather profound question in the hit, "Who Are You?" Pete Townsend wrote it over 30 years ago, and we hope CSI can finally bring him an answer.

Now, let's move on to a very elementary question. Who is the customer, and who is the customer service representative? You may be thinking, "What kind of bonehead doesn't know the difference?" And while I agree the question may be beneath you, I would argue, based on the answer to the first question in our pop quiz, roughly 40% of the people reading this book may struggle with the question. So let's address the issue: Who are you?

First, let's separate the roadies from the fans. There are two types of customers: internal and external.

Internal Customers: "I'm with the band, man…"

For our purposes, internal customers are all those that wear the school/district badge. They are the school district's finest. It may seem foolish to you, but when I was planning the Welcome Center for the Wake County Public School System, I never really considered the needs or the impact of our internal customers. Somebody much wiser than me suggested that internal customers, if not properly served, have both the ability and audacity to ruin my day.

No way! Surely, since we are on the same team, internal customers will cut me a little slack! Or so I thought.

Soon after we opened the new Center the first district-wide payday rolled around. Anyone here work in the Payroll Office? Let me tell you, when Mack the Knife doesn't feel his paycheck is accurate, it can get downright scary. I was introduced to a whole new vocabulary that day. So much for the patience of the internal customer. I learned quickly to prepare for my cohorts.

Just for kicks, sit down with a school secretary and ask him/her to describe their all-time worst customers. School frontliners love to tell stories of disgruntled internal customers. I'll bet many of you would prefer a nasty external customer over a nasty internal customer ten times out of ten! I sure would.

Some days, when dealing with ugly internal customers, I feel like the inspiration for the Green Day song She, *"Are you feeling like a social tool without a use?"*

External Customers: "I'm your number one fan!"

So who is left? You guessed it. Everyone else. External customers include students, parents, media, community members, potential newcomers, researchers, and the beat goes on. Obviously, you have many more potential external customers than internals. In fact, you can count your internals and know for sure the scope, but externals are unlimited and change daily – truly a moving target.

To this day, though I am now more attuned to my internal customers, I remain passionate about serving the external customers. The public relations function is what drives me. What beat do you dig? Do you relate more to the music or the lyrics? What drives you? Do you have a preference? Are you equally prepared to assist both types of customers?

Who are Customer Service Representatives?

Let me make one thing perfectly clear: if you are going to jump start a customer service revival in your school or district, you MUST find a way to remind – or convince – every employee of their unofficial title: *Customer Service Representative*. I don't care how high or low they happen to be on the food chain. We are all customer service representatives. Whether your badge says teacher, custodian, cashier, secretary, principal, bus driver or superintendent! Read my lips: YOU ARE A CUSTOMER SERVICE REPRESENTATIVE!

Whew! Rock on, Brother.

Have I made this point strong enough? In my district there are 17,000 Barney Fifes. We are all deputized as customer service representatives and authorized to provide world-class service. None of us is granted immunity to offering assistance. There are no Lone Rangers. It may have made for a popular Eagles song, but being a desperado will not work in a team sport like customer service.

It is crucial that all customer service representatives, that is, all employees, recognize the school district is not the buildings, the desks, the computers or the books. The school district is the people wearing the badge. It is all of us. We are music, and we write the songs. Therefore, I am the Wake County Public School System.

More importantly, the show doesn't end at 5:00! Huh? What I mean to say is I don't stop being the Wake County Public School System at 5:00. I cannot promote my district as an ambassador during the day and then badmouth my district after hours. I cannot stand in the grocery store line and talk "out of shop" about my principal or superintendent. Just for the record, NOTHING IS OFF THE RECORD! If you cannot become the school district, then do not accept the job. Unlike Rock 'n Roll, there is such a thing as bad publicity – and we want no part of it. Let the paparazzi chew on that for a while.

Whew! I know, Papa don't preach. Sorry. Can you sense my passion? Can I get an "Amen"?

It is also very important that all of us realize the burden and the **privilege we carry as the voice of the school district. We're all part of the band, whether singing lead or backup, and your voice carries.** The community reads articles about your district in the local newspaper, and they watch the evening news, but they *believe* what they hear from YOU. Why? Because you are the school district. You wear the badge. You are with the band.

To illustrate, a few years back a bond referendum failed to pass in my district. It was the first bond failure in the history of the school district. Not only did it fail, but it was voted down at a 2-1 clip. You could see the look of bewilderment on the faces of all those in the Superintendent's office the next day. How did this happen? How could the community not pass the bond? What did we do wrong? Interesting questions.

More interesting was the outcome of a second bond that was sent to the public for approval. This occurred about 18 months later but for a similar amount of money. The second bond passed – at nearly a 3-1 rate!

Two things happened in between the first and second referenda. First, the new Welcome Center was opened. I can't lay claim to the passing of the second bond, but they don't call me "Bond, Jeff Bond" for nothing. No, far more important was the hiring of a new superintendent with a very profound opinion of why the first bond failed. You see, he was on staff as an assistant superintendent and witnessed the failure first hand. So when he was named as the new leader, he claimed the bond failed for one reason: because our own crew of internal customers, our workforce, was not unified and educated about the need for the bond's approval.

He called his central office administrators into the board room one morning and offered a wonderful presentation. He put up slides that showed the actual and expected population growth as well as the potential impact on each school. He listed the number of mobile classrooms that would be needed at each site if the bond was to fail. He never told us how to vote, he simply educated us on the need for new and renovated schools.

Upon completion, we all cheered and said, "Yeah, that was great Mr. Superintendent" – for it was indeed. But he wasn't finished. He then pointed to a table in the back of the room. On it was a spreadsheet with each school in the district listed. We were instructed to sign our name next to two or three schools each. We were to call the principals of our assigned schools and arrange a time to make the same presentation to the faculty and staff. The slides were available for download on the intranet. Huh? You want me to do what?

It was eye-opening to say the least. The new superintendent believed that if our entire workforce was educated and unified, the public would believe what we had to say. It turns out he was right. I am now a believer that the badge carries more weight than the media. It is important that we pass this message along to ALL who wear it. Don't avoid the spotlight. Step into it and sing your song!

Show Time... Five Customer Needs

I understand about indecision
But I don't care if I get behind
People livin' in competition
All I want is to have my peace of mind

Peace of Mind - Boston

At the end of the day, all customers, whether internal or external, have the same five fundamental needs for peace of mind.

Ease Up On the Bouncers

1. All customers need to feel welcome. This is more than placing a cute little sign on your desk or a board-crafted pronouncement that "You matter to us." Those displays may be fine, but I am really suggesting the customer needs to feel welcome to approach YOU. In fact, the real test is whether or not he feels welcome to approach you a second time. Everyone can enter or call a school office to get assistance once. Many may not want to come back if the service is atrocious. But all customers need to know beyond any doubt that it is okay to approach YOU for further assistance. Will their interaction with you be like Elvis Presley's "Welcome To My World" or more like Alice Cooper's "Welcome To My Nightmare"?

The Voice of a Rocker, Heart of a Poet

2. All customers need to be understood. I have engaged in heart-to-heart conversations with staff members on multiple occasions to remind them the burden of understanding falls on the customer service representative and not on the customer. Sure, the customer can be of tremendous help in this process, but the ultimate responsibility is mine. I realize language and accents along with hostilities and emotions can become barriers, but strategies must be in place to get us to the point where we can understand the customer. Please do not waste my time pleading, "If the customer would have been able to explain it…" or, "If that's what she wanted, she should have just asked." I challenge all customer service representatives to have pre-established strategies for understanding and serving customers. Doesn't every shoe store in the mall have a plan for making a difficult sale? Shouldn't your school office? It requires teamwork.

Sometimes great misunderstandings between a customer and school official can be triggered by a slight misuse of a single word. For instance, my wife is from the South. I am not. It took me our first three years of marriage to realize when Lori claimed to be "ill", she was upset with me! I thought she just needed an Advil.

Often we get frustrated because of difficult communication, but do not take the time to involve a teammate who may be able to quickly decipher the customer's need and save everyone a headache (I wouldn't want us all to be ill).

R-E-S-P-E-C-T

3. All customers need to retain dignity. "How long before my dignity is reclaimed?" asks Alanis Morissette in her song, <u>Flinch</u>. Well to our dismay, it takes longer than we expect and sometimes it may never be reclaimed.

Until recently, my district's administration building, which houses the Welcome Center, also housed an employee from another department known for her less-than-stellar customer service. She truly did her part in maintaining the 37-43 rule. Fortunately, she is torturing our customers no longer. Perhaps she is in your district now. I'll call her Olga (isn't that Latin for "ugly monster"?).

How did I find out about her terrible customer service habits? From the security guard (yes, we have a security guard). I'll call him Brutus. You see, one summer, Brutus decided he was no longer content being a security guard in our administration building. Brutus, evidently, wanted to be a counselor. When angry customers stopped by his desk to check out and exit the building, instead of just signing them out and letting them go, Brutus would bring the huffing and puffing customer into the Welcome Center. Not only that, he would walk right past the counter and into my office with his new red-eyed, fire-breathing client. I could be in the middle of a project and hear the all-too-familiar deep voice say, "Jeff, this person is having a little trouble. Can you help him out?" Before I could stutter some excuse as to my heavy workload, Brutus would be gone, and I would be left with this customer who is burning holes into my forehead with his laser-like stare. How should I even begin this conversation? Typically, I might say "Good morning. Come on in. How can I help you today?" I might as well figure on a 45 minute conversation - minimum.

What amazed me about Brutus' clientele is the eerily similar tales they would tell. A very disproportionate number had just left Olga's office. I expected them to tell me she cussed at them or called them a name or some other unacceptable customer service (and social) no-no. Instead, they often surprisingly described the interaction and inevitably mentioned how she looked over her glasses at them. What? Are you kidding me? It is true, Olga often wore her glasses down near the tip of her beak, but I always assumed they were bifocals. Surely there must be a reason she wore them that way – not simply to talk down to customers. Truth be known, I don't think Olga was the worst customer service representative we have ever employed (I can remember one worse), but even if her intentions were good, customers perceived her actions as belittling. They felt as if they had just been to the principal's office.

We have to remember, many of our customers didn't enjoy a good school experience when they were students. They may have lamented about "smokin' in the boy's room" or chanted with glee, "school's out for summer, school's out forever." Many do not look forward to dealing with the school, even as parents. And they especially do not want to be anywhere near the district's administration building.

Olga, I admit, had a difficult job. She was in a position in which she had to rightfully deny many requests. However, her lack of polish and apparent power trips made customers furious. On top of that, she always seemed to enjoy a good brouhaha. The bottom line is she robbed customers of their dignity.

Help! I Need Somebody

4. All customers need to obtain assistance. I don't know about you, but I get zero customers calling, writing or visiting merely to confirm the school district is doing a marvelous job. I believe we have many members of our community who feel that way, but they typically do not take the time to call and let us know. The folks who do take the time to call are those possessing a need (and some may truly be possessed!). There is something they feel we can do to assist them. It may be they need some information, or they may want to offer some information.

One bad habit many of us fall into is that of making assumptions about customer needs. True, based on the season or the headlines on the morning news, we may get the same five or six questions all day long. But many of us fall into the habit of hearing a key word and then jumping in with the assistance we think the customer needs. It is crucial that we hear the entire question before we supply some autopilot answer. It may be the customer has a unique situation that is not like the previous 50 with which we have just dealt. If my beautiful and outspoken, er, I mean well-spoken wife was writing this section, she would be thrilled to interject that I could be a stronger customer service representative if only I was a better listener!

Perhaps Billy Idol stopped by his kid's school before he wrote Listen?

What's it like to play a part?
What's it like to have a wooden heart?
Every word you say is so rehearsed
You think your clothes and actions control the universe

And the Award Goes to …

5. All customers need to recognize their value. This book is not entirely about parent involvement, though I do have a serious interest in that topic and enjoy training teachers in that area. There are many ways to get parents into your schools. You can hire a new principal, make the staff wear mad mullet wigs or add a new science wing. Sure, parents will come once to see what's up. But (prepare to highlight this line) **to get positive, significant and sustained parental involvement, I propose you must have a strong commitment to excellent customer service.** Part of that commitment must include a component that emphasizes your appreciation for the opportunity to serve the customer. Every interaction should remind customers of their value. If you have a staff member who just doesn't get this concept, take him or her aside for some old-fashioned 'splainin'.

Just like students who know they are valued perform better academically and behaviorally, parents who know they are valued approach school from a positive perspective and contribute to the goals of the educational community.

One of my great joys is coaching my two daughters' softball teams. One year, we had a dad that I suspected was going to be a thorn in my side, second guessing all decisions and making known his dissatisfactions within earshot of the other parents. The other coach and

I took a two-step approach with him. First, we simply smothered him with kindness. We told him how well his daughter was doing and made a point to speak with him at each practice. We always smiled when conversing with him. Next, we asked him to give us a hand with one of the batting drills. After helping out a couple times, he quickly came on board and turned out to be a wonderful source of help. He became an official assistant coach. He was great with the kids and a real team guy. We were fortunate to have him.

As school people, we need to get similar positive involvement from our parents and our community. It will only happen if we take the initiative to let them know how much we value them.

I am human and I need to be loved
Just like anybody else does
How Soon Is Now? – The Smiths

Pet Peeves

I walk around pretending you were never here
But the smell of you is everywhere

Angry – Pat Benatar

Rock stars never have to worry about the little things that drive them batty (hidden Ozzie reference). They just have the manager add to the contract a rider that prohibits things they don't like and provides lots of the things that make them happy. Unfortunately, educators don't have this luxury. We do, however, still have those annoyance buttons, and probably quite a few. How do we handle it? What happens when customers push those tiny little hidden buttons? The buttons that send you into a crazed frenzy. The buttons that just set you off. Yeah, those buttons.

You probably think that you've got your act pretty well together and that you avoid going all "Courtney Love" on somebody over a minor infraction. Well, I would bet the proceeds of this book (at the time of writing, I still have hope someone other than my mom will buy a copy) that you have a button for small annoyances as well. The thing is, you may not even realize some of the small stuff that drains your tank.

As I ponder my own hot button issues, I have come to recognize two customer habits that drive me nuts. The first is when a customer **calls in for information and I fully understand the need and prepare to respond.** As I begin to share what I deem as the perfect answer, the customer interrupts with, "Oh. Hold on a minute. I need to go find a pen and paper."

KABOOM! The customer, WHO CALLED ME FOR INFORMATION, is looking for a writing utensil. And it never fails, the pen they bring to the phone doesn't work. They need to go find another. Meanwhile, I am busy jamming paper clips into my eyeballs. Of course there are three more callers in queue and a line of customers standing at my desk as well. Ugggh! And as for the pen, I can't remember having a pen "run dry" in the past eighteen years. How is it that every customer has a pen run dry at the very moment I am providing the information FOR WHICH THEY CALLED??? In fact, at every phone in my house and at my office, I have a bunch of pens, usually in a cup. There is never just one pen, the pens cling together like a school of fish. Maybe I'm not normal (go ahead and say it). Maybe it is the norm to have to go searching for a pen and then have it dry up at the very moment it is needed. The fact that you found just one pen, all by itself, likely means it was separated from the group because it no longer functions. Throw it away. Keep working pens by the phone.

Whew. I know you're glad that's over. Sorry for the rant. But it truly is a pet peeve, and it is **MY** job to overcome it because customers will always be unprepared for the answers they get – whether it be with a pen and paper or with the actual information provided.

Another pet peeve of mine is one that I've only recently discovered. I have now realized, after years of answering this type of question, that all those people calling me to get the phone number of a school in our district had to look up the district's administration number in the phone book in order to call me. I know they didn't have me on their speed dial, nor did they have my number memorized. *They looked it up!* Duh! Why didn't they just look up the school number? I feel like screaming, "Ricky don't lose that number, it's the only one you want…"

Okay, okay. I won't rant too long on this one. But you get the idea.

So, what are your peeves? Do you like it when customers make references to "you people"? As in "You people need to get your act together." This can be especially frustrating if you pride yourself on being a great employee and you get lumped in by sweeping generalizations. "You people" can turn us off even when a compliment is intended.

Or do you get tweaked when a customer uses language that you choose not to include in your vocabulary? Do you have a hard time working with a customer that obviously feels more important than you? I'll bet you love it when you provide accurate information in response to a customer question only for him to respond with, "Who else can I speak with?"

Another of my favorites is when a newcomer tells us how things would be so much better if we would function more like her superior school district back in (insert location) the land of milk and honey from which she recently departed.

I'm sure we could go on and on. I enjoy this part of the class in a live training event. Participants typically have more pet peeves than we have time to discuss. The live rants are especially entertaining. If you were sleeping during the first half hour, you are awake and participating now!

Hopefully, none of the above would classify as big deals. However, if I allow myself to get ticked off about little things, I may offer the customer less than excellent service - and **that will not be the fault of the customer!** It is important that I do not write off a customer simply because I find him to be an annoyance. I cannot disregard the fundamental needs of a customer because she pushed one of my buttons.

After all, the Grateful Dead taught us, "Ain't no time to hate, barely time to wait."

Customers, with all their button-pushing habits, tend to find us. It is the nature of the customer service industry. We cannot pick and choose which customers we will serve. No, we will serve all who walk through our door. And, somehow, they all find their way to our door.

The long and winding road / That leads to your door / Will never disappear
I've seen that road before / It always leads me here / Leads me to your door
<u>The Long and Winding Road</u> - The Beatles

I challenge you to handle your buttons with the utmost professionalism, and do not let them compromise your own customer service excellence. Better yet, figure out a way to get rid of those buttons altogether!

"No Soup For You!"
(Bad Service)

Cool is a rule, but sometimes bad is bad

Bad is Bad – Huey Lewis and the News

Television sitcoms are loaded with humorous examples of bad customer service. I can find none more hilarious than *Seinfeld's* Soup Nazi – though his car rental experience (Year 3, Episode 11) was a close second. Surely, you have seen or at least heard friends and co-workers referring to "No Soup For You!" We like to laugh at the character's lack of customer service, **BUT** I'm afraid the actor in the show is playing a role too often found in our schools.

You see, the Soup Nazi had this wonderful product – his famous soup recipes – but he created all these unnecessary rules and enforced them with brutal rigidity. His rules were for the benefit of himself and not his customers. Do you have rules that benefit yourself or your office, but not the customer? Look hard. ... Look *harder*. I'll bet there are a few in there.

Now, don't get me wrong, I like rules. In fact, I'm quite neurotic about following the rules. However, I have recently started examining the rules in my own office to look for inapplicable or outdated mandates. For instance, our Office of Student Assignment is responsible for all student placements and oversees the student transfer request process. In years past, only the original transfer request forms were accepted. That meant a parent could not fax one to them.

So why not accept a faxed request form? It was probably a rule that was implemented years ago and has outlived its original purpose. Recently, in what I deemed a great customer-friendly move, the Office of Student Assignment began accepting faxed copies. This has saved both parents and administrators much heartache.

In my training classes, I like to take a few minutes to encourage participants to share stories of bad customer service. This is advantageous for many reasons. First, it gets everyone thinking. It also gets many of our "I-do-not-want-to-be-here-but-my-boss-thinks-I-need-training-in-customer-service" types involved in the conversation. Until this point they have been sitting with their arms crossed waiting for me to give them a reason to refocus their angst my way. Most importantly, it provides me with many examples, real-life examples, to which I can refer as we move through the day's material. Oh, the songs I could write!

My most memorable experience with this activity occurred in a class I was teaching to personnel from my own school district. The class was made up of folks from a variety of central office departments as well as frontliners from multiple schools. We probably had close to 20 people in a fairly small room.

After all the stories were shared, the final story came from a guy that I knew as a customer service shining star. Rich shared that on his way over to the class, he stopped at Wal-Mart to pick up some batteries. It was early in the morning and hardly anyone was in the store. He approached the check-out line and was pleasantly surprised to see the store representative wearing a badge that said, "Customer Service Manager". He thought to himself, "How nice. I'm on my way to a customer service class, and I am going to get a terrific example from a customer service professional."

Guess again. Rich went on to explain that she simply scanned his batteries and, in a voice suggesting she didn't care to be serving him, then said, "Seven, forty-five." She never greeted him, asked him if he found everything he was looking for, or thanked him.

"Seven, forty-five." Are you kidding me? That would be an awful story if it ended there. But that was just the beginning. As he was sharing this horrid service example, a class participant from another department loudly interrupted with rage in her voice, "But you don't know what she's going through. Maybe she's having trouble at home. Maybe she has financial issues…."

Rich would have none of it. He calmly let her know, in no uncertain terms, the Wal-Mart representative needed to separate her personal troubles, if that was indeed the issue, from her customer relations performance. And he was right.

At this point, I felt like I was hosting my own talk show – competition for Jerry Springer. You see, the lady interrupting and defending the store clerk was also known throughout the district as being our very own Customer Service Public Enemy Number One. She was clearly the worst customer service representative I have ever seen in a school district or any other line of work. Fortunately, she is no longer frustrating the fine folks of Wake County, North Carolina. She was continually rude and consistently short with customers. And, frankly, she was really scary. Kind of like The Kink's "Lola" scary!

While that particular class went down in my personal customer service training hall of fame as one of the most memorable, it is important that after sharing our stories of bad service we delve into the *causes* of bad service. Like mentioned in the Pop Quiz chapter, we must be diligent about pinpointing the causes of bad service before we can prescribe a solution. I have often thought it would be fun to dedicate some time during our training sessions to break the class into groups and have each group devise a list of bad service causes – not excuses, but legitimate reasons.

Never fear, in an effort to move things along, your favorite author has created a list of four actions or inactions (or *mis*actions if that is a word) that I believe to be major contributors to poor service habits.

Take me to the station / And put me on a train
I've got no expectation / To pass through here again
No Expectations – The Rolling Stones

1. **Expectations.** This, in my expert opinion, is a very common contributor to bad service. In any department, school or district, quality customer service begins with the top dog. It is not a grass roots phenomenon. Allow me to take it one step further. Here's a strong statement that may draw your ire:

Show me a consistently rude school secretary, and I'll show you a school principal that doesn't give a flying flip about customer service!

The example should be set by leadership, and the expectations must be clear and consistent. Staff should know the deal before they ever show up for their first day of work. Be sure the customer service expectations are written. There should be no guessing as to what is expected.

You who are on the road must have a code that you can live by
Teach Your Children – Graham Nash

2. **Training.** Frontliners are often trained in easily-measured skills such as payroll procedures, bookkeeping standards and student registrations. However, I have yet to meet the school or district that trains new staff in how to treat customers. Who ever said to a new hire, "Here is how I want you to treat parents," or how about, "This is the climate we want to create for our community?" Unfortunately, it is difficult to get them away from

the office once they begin the new job. I would like to see more districts offer customer service training (really good customer service training) as part of the new hire orientation. I want the rookies to have this training before showing up for work in their new office. Frankly, in my perfect world, all district personnel would complete this training prior to reporting for duty. What a climate that could create. As John Lennon said, "Imagine"!

We must not fall into the siren song of complacency. Some districts do not get many customer complaints (note, I did not say they are necessarily offering quality service) and, therefore, do not feel a need for an ongoing customer service training program. One of the nation's largest school districts recently told me customer service training was not a topic it was addressing because they "just did customer service training three years ago."

Double WOW! I strongly encourage all schools and districts to implement a customer service training program for new hires, and a regularly scheduled refresher course for all district personnel.

Who's to blame for my mistakes?
<u>Drift And Die</u> – Puddle of Mudd

3. **Hiring.** This is a tricky one. We all think we are experts when it comes to making personnel selections. However, hiring the wrong person to carry your banner can lead to serious problems. As we all know, it is quite difficult to get rid of a bad employee in a school system. Unless she steals money or pinches someone, she will likely be there, ruining life for you and everyone else, for 30 years. You'll be like Meatloaf, "praying for the end of time to hurry up and arrive." So here are some hints about hiring strong customer service representatives.

The first rule of thumb is this: if they don't smile at the interview, don't expect them to smile on the job! When conducting an interview, I like to have the candidate wait in the lobby for just a minute or two. I want to know if he treats the frontline customer service representative stationed in the lobby with the same kindness shown to me. When I come out of my office to retrieve the candidate, I want to see him showing off his "poop-eatin' grin" (learned that one from my poker buddies) as he reaches out to shake my hand. In fact, he should be smiling before a single word is spoken. I expect a tremendous first impression on the part of the candidate. I try to provide the same.

Next, I have no intention of recommending someone for hire based on *what she knows*. I will, however, recommend someone for hire based on *who she is*. Edie Brickell sang "What I am is what I am, are you what you are or what?" Like Edie, I am interested in the real person – the person behind the mask.

Please do not try to impress me with the fact that you worked in a school for 20 years in another state. I also don't care that you have a CPA, MBA, JD, EdD, or any other letters after your name. All of those qualities may be helpful in the event you are ranked dead even with another candidate, but none of those things make you qualified if you score a big goose egg in the character category. Way too many frontliners conduct themselves as if they are doing the customer a favor. I refuse to add to that pool of confusion. While interviewing, I am less inclined to pay attention to what you are saying and more likely attuned to how you say it. Again, the impression you make at the interview will be the impression you are expected to make on a daily basis.

As educators we believe that all children can learn. Right? Of course we do. That is a correct statement, and we will go to our grave defending the ideal. Rightly so! However, I must then ask the follow up question. Do you believe all adults can learn? Hmmm. Philosophically, I have to say yes, or else the aforementioned ideal concerning all children may prove contradictory. So, while I do hesitantly assert (and I'm sure each of us is struggling with a vision of some adult we know that would challenge this notion) that all adults can learn, I also believe it would not be prudent to hire a non-service-oriented person. Sure, they could learn to be strong customer service representatives, but if it takes 27 years of training just to get three good years out of them before retirement…I would not call that a positive return on investment.

When I was a rookie school administrator, I found myself amazed at the existing mode of operations at my school. It seemed that every morning, after the pledge and morning announcements, the teacher assistants would come to the work room, which was directly across the hall from my office, and wait in long lines to make copies. I watched this for a few days and quickly discovered that it was actually social time. As you can imagine, this ticked me off! There were children in my school who could not read, and these assistants wanted to spend 20 minutes making copies of something they probably did not need anyway? That practice had to change.

So I made a very unpopular, but (as I still believe to this day) wise decision. I searched for a teacher assistant with less-than-stellar customer skills. Unfortunately, it turns out there were quite a few who fit the criteria. So, I chose that special someone and made her the "copy lady". The other teacher assistants were instructed to bring their copies to her, and she would have them ready for pickup later in the day. This new procedure solved two problems. It got the copy lady away from people, **AND** it caused the others to get back in the classroom. I know, I know, you are thinking that was a bit harsh, especially for the new guy, but I brought the idea to my supervisor before announcing it, and she seemed to think it was very appropriate. So there! My point in all this is to say bad service can often be the result of poor hiring by management – and maybe by previous management regimes even (in the case of my no-service teacher assistant) from a previous decade.

4. **Rules.** I was recently studying the Nordstrom method for offering superstar customer service. After all, Nordstrom employees appear to be the standard by which all others are measured. I found it interesting that they draft policies purposely promoting service excellence. They try to avoid a lot of the minutia and detailed job specifications that can become so petty and repressive. Instead, they hire good people and get out of their way. They trust their folks to use good sense, and they back the decisions of the representatives. Who among us would like to work in that environment? Yeah, thought so.

Unfortunately, many of us work in settings which include lists of rules longer than ZZ Tops' beards. Frequently, rules are made without any regard for customer service impact. I can think of some rules and policy decisions that have made customer service very difficult. I bet you can too. Perhaps we should follow the advice of the wise old motivational speaker/pop legend, Michael Jackson, "When the world is on your shoulder, got to straighten up your act and boogie down."

Not that I consider myself a complainer or a difficult customer, but lately I have been trying to cut some degree of slack for those in the airlines industry. I recognize the number of rules has increased in recent years, and customer service may be significantly more complicated than in years past. However, competition for air travel market share is strong. The airlines, in general, are a great example of taking difficult rules and maintaining standards of customer service excellence.

To sum up my thoughts about poor customer service, I believe the guilty fall into one or more of the following four categories:

1) They do not have clear expectations/examples from leadership;

2) They are not equipped with the proper training;

3) They should not have been hired in the first place (ouch!);

4) The organization is set up to fail

Bad service is all around us. We recognize it when we are the customers. We even recognize it in our co-workers. Unfortunately, we rarely see it in our own habits. Yogi Berra once said, "You can observe a lot by just watching." I encourage you to devote extra attention to your own customer service performance. Go ahead and look closely at the dressing room mirror. To take it further, find a colleague, co-worker, supervisor or even a trusted customer and ask him to watch you closely over the next two weeks and offer honest feedback. Like a colonoscopy, it may cause some much-needed humility, but eventually you will be glad to have endured it.

All I want is everything

Am I asking too much?

<u>All I Want Is Everything</u> – Def Leppard

Common Shortfalls

I wish that I could push a button
And talk in the past and not the present tense
And watch this hurtin' feeling disappear
Like it was common sense
It was a fine idea at the time
Now it's a brilliant mistake

Brilliant Mistake – Elvis Costello

You dream about it, hope it will happen, then one day you make it: You're a headliner! No more warming up the crowd for the main act. Your name is in lights! That's how I felt when I was handed the reigns as the lead customer service guy in a very large school district. And like all new leaders, I quickly discovered some areas needing major attention. I figured the problems were specific to my district. However, as I began meeting regularly with directors of communications from other school districts around North Carolina, I learned that my district was not alone in our customer service battles. Apparently "we are the world." I am fully convinced these are universal problems.

So, I started my own band, so to speak, and with the spirit of an entrepreneur, an idea popped into my overly-optimistic mind. I decided to establish a corporation that would perform customer service audits. I figured they would be similar to communications audits, except specifically focused on the single element of customer service. I convinced a colleague to enter this venture with me and we created a consulting firm called Turning Point Solutions, Inc.

At first we were simply hoping to help some of our neighboring school districts by conducting customer service audits locally. At that time, we had no idea of the coast-to-coast need for this type of product. However, a few years and many school districts later, we are now a national company with staff stationed around the country. Can you say "road trip"? Very soon after opening, we began getting requests to train school and district staff as well as audit. We now spend as much of our time training as we do auditing. Imagine that!

I have learned many interesting things on tour – things I could not learn in my own district. Each school and district with which I work is unique. The individuals that make up each team combine to form a culture that is distinctive, like a fingerprint. And while it would be foolish to paint all of these cultures with a broad stroke, it is feasible to look for trends. I am careful not to assume the trends are perfect correlations and in no way will I implore the notion of one size fits all. However, I have noticed a few customer service problems that seem to pop up more frequently, and I want to share them with you. As you read them, you can nod in affirmation as if to say, "Yep, that's my school all right." Or maybe you can shake your head and say, "Thank goodness we don't have that issue." Either way, I encourage you to consider them a checklist. Ask yourself if any of these stumbling blocks currently impact your community.

Reaching a "Live" Person

> *Tell me in a world without pity*
> *Do you think what I'm askin's too much?*
> *I just want something to hold on to*
> *And a little of that human touch*
>
> Human Touch – Bruce Springsteen

Considering that our chosen industry caters to the most important possession of any family, its offspring, it is amazing to think a parent can call during the hours we are responsible for said sweetness and not get to talk to someone. True, many of the "emergency" calls a school receives are things that could wait until later, but the mere fact that a parent cannot speak with a frontliner is an enormous problem.

This is a great example of an issue that I thought was specific to my district. I was floored to learn it goes on across the land on a daily basis. I have found in many cases, surely not all cases, that smaller, more rural schools and districts are likely to have a phone answered by a receptionist and not a machine during the school day. Obviously, if we compare a school of 300 students with a school of 900 students, both with a front office consisting of only a receptionist and a data manager, the smaller school will likely get less customers and therefore can provide more accessibility to each customer.

As you can guess, I hear all the time from school frontliners screaming "You don't know what it's like in my office. I cannot possibly be on the phone and still distribute thermometers, sign in tardy students, listen to hypersensitive parents, etc."

Yes, I do know what your office is like. And, no, I do not expect you to answer the phone at the cost of accomplishing other, more important tasks. How should we prioritize the phone calls versus the walk-in customers versus the e-mail inbox? I will address those a little later. For now, I would argue this problem is not a frontliner issue. It is an administrative issue. If the phones are not being answered by a live person, then the principal needs to devise a solution.

Central office folks are not "off the hook" on this one (get it?). The whole purpose of a central office is to ensure the success of its schools. If a school employee cannot get a live person at the central office, then we find a problem in need of immediate attention. Jackson Browne hit it right on the nose when he sang, "My problem is you, waiting here for you."

Inconsistent Information

I exploit you / Still you love me
I tell you one and one makes three
Cult of Personality – Living Colour

Would you like to have some fun? Tomorrow, after school gets up and running, select a school district, either your own or that of a friend, call ten of their schools and ask each (assuming you get to speak with a live person) to list the documents you need to register your child. I'll bet you get at least five different answers to that question. Expect to find differing opinions as to what constitutes proof of residence. Regarding the birth certificate, some will demand a certified copy, others may accept a mother's copy. You get the point.

This *should* be an easy fix, but it is not. We have a rule in my office that goes "If you can't find it in writing, don't say it!" The solution could be to put everything – EVERYTHING – on the district website so that all school personnel are referring to the same data containment area and drawing upon the same information. In fact, many districts do a great job of keeping necessary items online and frequently updated. Often the breakdown seems to lie with the frontliner that is not properly trained to use the website or does not spend enough time perusing the district site. However, in all fairness, many other times the frontliner is very astute, but the information on the district site is outdated and inaccurate. This is a grievous error.

Periodically, I create scavenger hunts for my staff in which they have to use our website to find the answers. I try to find obscure information from pages that are rarely, if ever, viewed by anyone other than our webmaster. I do this not because I care for them to memorize this stuff. Rather, I want them to know how to find it, and I want them to stumble upon some "a-ha" stuff along the way.

Distributing bad information is worse than giving no information at all. The tricky part is, in the school business, the information can change daily – even hourly! It is crucial that we keep on top of it.

Return Messages

Sent me an e-mail with all the details
Sent Me An E-mail – J-Shin

The act of leaving messages, whether a voicemail or e-mail or handwritten "while you were out," is an important part of customer service and communications in general. In fact, many times I prefer to leave a message rather than actually talk with someone. The procedure is quick and painless. The problems begin with the return messages. You see, they are often delayed and sometimes non-existent. This practice causes all kinds of dilemmas for the guy waiting on the return message.

Again, have some fun. Create a dummy e-mail account with Yahoo or Hotmail or any of the free services. Send messages to a bunch of people on varying levels of the totem pole. See how long it takes to get a message back. Are there some that never respond? This is a scary exercise because you might not like the results. Also, you might wonder if a co-worker is reading this book and e-mailing you undercover. Perhaps you should take a break from reading and go check your inbox!

How much time am I allotted to return a message? Typically, 24 hours is acceptable. That is not to say I must have an answer within 24 hours, but I must, at a minimum, make a return contact to let the caller/writer know I have received the message and am working on a solution. People are generally pleased with that kind of service. As long as you acknowledge their need and let them know you are on the case, they will show some degree of patience while you work for resolution.

Rushed Tone

Yeah, if you're moving too fast
Won't you want it to last
You better walk it, talk it
You better walk it as you talk it or you lose that beat
<u>Walk & Talk</u> – Velvet Underground

One day at a staff meeting, I thought it would be fun to try an exercise with my staff. I divided the nation into regions and assigned each member of my team a region. After we determined Delaware is not in the Midwest as well as other geographical miscues, I challenged each person to go online and locate three large school districts from their assigned region. Then I instructed them to call the district office and simply ask a question – any question. You can, if you like, pretend you are a newcomer to the area and get information. Perhaps you want to know how to get a job in that district. I told them we would come back together next week and share our findings. They left the meeting excited. One said "Good. This will be fun!"

The following week, we gathered, and I noticed gloomy faces. I asked what was wrong, and the same co-worker stated, "That exercise was horrible!" When we went around the table sharing our experiences, we reached a quick consensus that many districts are customer service challenged.

I, too, called three large districts. Two of them offered voicemail messages with promises of a returned call. Years later, I am still waiting by my phone. I feel like Ricky Lee Jones in <u>Flying Cowboys</u> when he sang, "Who can I turn to? Who can I trust?" Maybe today will be the day!

My third call, however, was answered by a live person. She was obviously trying to get me off the line. She really wanted to transfer me to her technology department, though my questions had nothing to do with that topic. I finally asked her if she had another incoming call. She confirmed there were multiple calls in queue. It was a disheartening experience for both of us. I was disappointed in the service, or lack thereof, provided by her district. The customer service representative was no doubt disappointed in her own lack of ability to serve my needs due to her school district's organizational structure. A textbook lose-lose situation.

Frontliner Not an Advocate

But to wait for you, is all I can do / And that's what I've got to face
Take a good look at me now / 'Cause I'll still be standing here
And you coming back to me is against all odds
It's the chance I've gotta take
<u>Against All Odds</u> – Phil Collins

I have experienced way too many school and district frontliners that, for some unbeknownst reason, believe they are the gatekeepers of information for a school or department. Perhaps they see their role as that of the school's very own news anchor? They are like Billy Joel's Big Shot. All their "friends were so knocked out!" Their tone makes it quite clear they will only share the information with me if I somehow prove myself worthy.

Must I always slay a dragon?

There are two ways customer service representatives can approach their jobs. Check this out:

1. I will *send* you to a solution for your problem.
2. I will *take* you to a solution for your problem.

The difference between the two seems very subtle, but in reality is enormous. A simple shift in paradigm from the former to the latter can make a world of difference in both the attitude and habits of the customer service representative.

Taking a customer to their solution implies going with them and staying with them until completion. I realize it sounds time consuming, however it can be accomplished in many cases without having to invest extra time. There are strategies available during the initial conversation that will assure the customer you are his advocate. More on this later.

Underutilization of Technology

The problem's plain to see / Too much technology
Machines to save our lives / Machines dehumanize
<u>Mr. Roboto</u> - Styx

I am not all geeked out over automating all of our customer service functions. It is true that sometimes technology can take away the "Human Touch," however, there are a couple areas we can provide better service by using available machines.

First, as mentioned earlier, **we need to make better use of our websites**. Many schools and districts do not utilize their website as the clearinghouse for all information. Additionally, frontliners should identify some other helpful sites to be bookmarked and readily available. In my office, we look at the leading television news station's website as well as the city's primary daily newspaper's website. Each morning upon beginning our day, we take a moment to scan the headlines. Whether correctly or incorrectly reported, the news about our schools will drive the questions, and we need to know what the public is thinking. Other bookmarked sites may include your state's Department of Education and a national news site such as cnn.com for when breaking stories of national significance occur.

Another misused technology tool is voicemail. I will speak to it more in our section on customer service via telephone. However, night service voicemail can be a wonderfully effective and inexpensive way to get information to your customers. First, you must decide if you want to have yours set up as a harbor for messages to be left overnight. In my shop, we have decided not to enable customers to leave messages overnight. However, prior to establishing the night service recording, we asked our local phone company to run a study to determine the number of attempted calls during a one week period between 5:00 pm and 8:00 am. Surprisingly, there were over 200 attempted calls! That fact alone indicated a great need for some type of informational recording that can be accessed by callers unable to dial during our operating hours.

Once we knew there was a market for the informational recording, we then needed to decide which information to include. Currently, and this is a never-ending revision process, if you call our school district after hours you will be greeted and asked if you would like to continue in English or Spanish. Next, you can get information about applying for a job, registering a student, etc. Each of those options has multiple selections as well. Ultimately, once narrowed down to the specific question, a thorough answer is available. I know many people get frustrated with phone trees, but as opposed to having no night service, we think it is pretty helpful – especially because it is easy to change. If bad weather rolls in during the middle of the night, and school gets cancelled or delayed, I can call in from home and change the message. People in our community know the message is updated as soon as the Superintendent makes the decision. It is another way for them to get up-to-date information.

Rock Star Status
(Good Service)

Welcome to my world
Won't you come on in?
Miracles I guess
Still happen now and then
Step into my heart
Leave your cares behind
Welcome to my world
Built with you in mind

<u>Welcome To My World</u> – Elvis Presley

A fully-stocked stretch limo pulls up to the Plaza Hotel in New York City to pick up you and your band for the start of your world tour at Madison Square Garden. As the limo slides next to the curb you see your name in lights, thousands of screaming fans and dozens of people to attend to your every need. Oh, yeah. It's good to be a rock star. Wouldn't it be great if our customers felt like that?

The Cars sang, "Let the good times roll" and that is certainly great advice for customer service frontliners. Most of the remainder of this book will be practical tips for strong service. The goal is for customer service representatives to develop great service habits. Anyone can offer great service when a board member or other quasi-celebrity walks through the door, but the true test lies in the ability to offer great service to the common man – and on a consistent basis. Remember our pop quiz?

I know we already finished our pet peeve chapter, but this is an appropriate time to register one more of my petty hang-ups. Perhaps this has happened to you. I call a school in my own district and meet up with a customer service interaction which I would deem less than stellar. However, once I introduce myself, I can hear the frontliner sort of straighten herself up while the tone of her voice changes. Now she is friendly and attentive! Are you kidding me?

OH, NO YOU DON'T! Do not treat me differently because you now know who I am. You continue on with the same poor service. **I get highly offended by frontliners who offer different levels of service depending upon the hierarchy of the customers.** This form of discrimination is more common than one might think.

I was recently brought into a meeting with a large school district in Virginia. The communications team and many of the cabinet members of this district recognized the huge need for customer service revival. We were asked to make a presentation outlining the steps we would implement, as consultants, to improve the manner of service provided. Upon conclusion of the meeting, everyone was excited to get started. I mean they were ready to jump in with both feet. Everyone except one man – the superintendent. He stood up and proclaimed there was no customer service problem in his district. Every school he visited was offering magnificent service. You should have read the faces of his staff. To this day, I cannot decide if they were merely disappointed or totally bewildered.

There were clearly two problems with his statement. First, he never had to deal with the "messes" caused by poor service. Staff members were already in place to address the complaints and filter out the solvable quandaries before they reached his desk. In his mind there was no issue. The other problem was simply the fact he was THE SUPERINTENDENT. Because he was the leader of the organization, of course the red carpet was rolled out for him wherever he went. To make matters worse, this guy was about 6'5" tall and a former football player. He just naturally commanded attention when he entered a room.

My point is we all have the know-how to provide excellent customer service. It's not rocket surgery! The hard part is instilling excellent service as a habit – time and time again, regardless of the stature of the customer. Below are five basic rules for developing strong customer service habits.

Always Be On Time

All night on the phone
What were you talking 'bout
You know I believe everything you have said
Broken Promise – Immature

By this, I do not mean punching the clock and sitting at your desk at 8:00 am sharp. Don't get me wrong, punctuality is not a bad thing. In fact, it is very important. But I'm talking about being on time with the promises you make. If, for instance, you tell someone you will have an answer for them by 3:00, then calling them at 3:05 is a broken promise. Yes, it sounds petty. However, in the words of Bruce Hornsby: "That's just the way it is."

Take it one step further. Whenever possible, over-deliver on your promises. Your customer will be ecstatic if you promise him you will have it by 3:00 and then you call him at 1:00. Wow! Rock Star service. You have just won a customer for life.

Offer Choices

We control the data banks
We control the think tanks
We control the flow of air
<u>We R In Control</u> - Neil Young

Choices are a great tool and should be used by the skilled customer service representative whenever feasible. Let's face it. When watching television with a group, we each like to be the one holding the clicker. There is a certain freedom, even a sense of power, which accompanies the ability to make decisions, and we all crave it. As a customer service representative, I would do well to offer that freedom to my clients.

This is especially helpful when dealing with customers suffering from Bullyitis. You know the type. They feel a need to bully the frontliner. They need to be in *total* control of *every* conversation at *all* times. You probably have other names for them (be nice). Here's the deal, providing them choices gives them the impression they are in control because they get to make decisions. But who is really in control? Me.

I am in control because I choose the options from which the bully can select. Of course there are limits. I am only going to provide him with options that are satisfactory to me…sort of like Elvis when he exclaimed, *"You can do anything, but stay off of my blue suede shoes."*

Let's take a real-life example. A disgruntled resident in my community calls with rage in her voice because the school bus ran over her mailbox (you think I make up this stuff?). She is furious and absolutely insists on controlling our interaction. I quickly assess that she needs a claim form from our Office of Risk Management. Being the astute customer service representative that I am, I soothe her angst by providing three choices.

I will be happy to mail the form to her, and she will get it in a couple days. If she prefers, I will gladly fax it to her, and she can have it by lunchtime. Finally, it will be my privilege to e-mail it to her, and she can have it in the next fifteen minutes.

The customer is happy because she gets to hold the remote. I am happy because I remained in control of the situation and implemented a win-win resolution. Notice I never gave her a choice that would cause me grief. I offered to mail, fax or e-mail the form to her. These are functions that I perform on a daily basis anyhow. Never did I offer to staple it to my forehead and crawl over to her house with it, though that would make a cool music video.

Keep Customers The Priority

What if I made some time to listen to you?
What if I made some time to hear me, too?
What If We Was Cool? – Eric Benet

Let me make this short and sweet: if the document on your desk, or the deadline looming, or the stack of papers needing to be filed takes precedent over assisting a customer, then you have crossed the line, and your service has become "bad to the bone." **Hear me clearly, I am not de-emphasizing the significance of those other duties.** However, like all other areas of life, we may be forced to make choices between two very important responsibilities. I am suggesting you choose to serve the customer before serving any other obligation.

And speaking of priorities, when choosing between customers, the order goes like this: the walk-in visitor gets served immediately (after all, he went to the greatest effort to interact with you, and there is no voicemail option with a face-to-face conversation); the telephone caller gets next priority; and the e-mail sender gets last priority (simply because it can be done after hours if necessary).

Keeping customers *the* priority is a real lesson in both focus and discipline. In fact, it would be a wonderful addendum to any school or district mission statement. Consider the parallel message in Boston's To Be A Man, *"What does it take to be a man? The will to give and not receive, the strength to say what you believe, the heart to feel what others feel."*

Please don't read any further until you have contemplated the preceding paragraph.

Be Accessapproachable

Beth, I know you're lonely
And I hope you'll be alright
'Cause me and the boys will be playin' all night
<u>Beth</u> – Kiss

Is that a remarkable word or what? Like any great song writer or poet, I feel free to make up words to fit my need. It's de-lovely! Feel free to use it on your next spelling test. I created it for use in customer service training. A few years ago, I used to preach the value of ***accessibility***. Too many people, particularly those with impressive titles, prevent the rest of us from being able to reach them. You hear conversations like:

"Don't give her my e-mail address."

"Why not?"

"She might send me an e-mail."

What? It sounds crazy but too many people are living deep within their forts. They seem to forget the part of their job that makes them <u>public</u> servants. The public pays for those phones and e-mail accounts. Now, I understand the superintendent's need for a phone line that is not constantly tied up with unfounded complaints and unsolicited opinions. However, I would argue too many of us non-superintendent types put up barriers that cause more problems than they prevent.

Have you ever received a call from a director (or higher) seeking a piece of information that you can provide? I sure have. Being a good frontliner, I tell her I do not have the information but I know where to find it and will call back in ten minutes. Then, as promised, I return the call in less than ten minutes. Lo and behold, I do not get the director. I get her secretary! She could have at least said, "Have your people call my people."

She did not even give *me* her direct contact information though she initiated the call! I find that amazing. It is not like I plan to write her number on the men's bathroom wall, "For a good time call…" I simply wanted to return her call and give her the information **SHE REQUESTED**.

> *Whatever that your days may bring*
> *No use hiding in a corner that won't change a thing*
> <u>In The Evening</u> – Led Zeppelin

So, inaccessibility is a problem. However, to the contrary, I bet we can all think of someone who claims, "My door is always open." Yet, when you leave his office you are scratching your head and thinking to yourself, "I do not want to deal with him anymore." Perhaps you are tired of being barked at or maybe even talked to like an inferior being.

This is where ***approachability*** comes into play. What good is being accessible if not simultaneously approachable? Hence, I created my own word: accessapproachable. It is important that we exhibit both traits and commit them to habit. I challenge each reader to examine your own work patterns. Do not be fooled into thinking this is an issue only impacting leaders. All of us need to monitor our accessibility and approachability. I can think of many central office and school representatives for whom this is a struggle. One frontliner demonstrating abysmal tendencies in either of these areas can undo years of work constructing a community-friendly reputation.

Dwell In The Realm Of Logic

> *Try to be a logical man*
> *Tryin' to help the world around me*
> <u>Only Love</u> – Hall & Oats

Remember the example of the lady whose mailbox was run over by a school bus mentioned earlier in this chapter? She was clearly living in the realm of emotion. That's okay for her. In fact, it is expected. But it is not okay for the customer service representative to get caught up in the realm of emotion when assisting a customer. I know it can be difficult, but you must remain in the realm of logic.

If you cross over into the realm of emotion, likely one of two scenarios will play out. First, you could take on the role of the customer's personal attorney. You might catch yourself saying something to the effect of:

"You're right, honey. This is a travesty. We're going to march right into the principal's office and get this straightened out…"

I am going to guess that is not the approach you want to take (all the principals reading are letting loose a collective "Amen" about now). Never convince yourself you are immune to this type of mama bear protectiveness. We all get our heartstrings tugged by an emotional customer now and then. It can overcome us in a very subtle manner. Before you know it, you are overstepping the boundaries and setting yourself up for a gigantic faux pas.

The other, and likely more common, scenario occurs when the customer service representative crosses over into the realm of emotion and becomes defensive. Admit it, you are guilty of having made this transition right before the eyes of a customer and so am I. This reactionary blunder often ends up on the superintendent's desk. Avoid at all costs.

One emotion
It's all over the place
You let it get out
It cuts in your face
<u>One Emotion</u> – The Clash

Three Genres of Service

When will I see you?
How will I know?
My voice echoes on
As I wait by the telephone
Maybe you'll be there
After the show
But hope slowly fades
Like the lights in a stage show

Guitar Blues – The Barclay James Harvest

There may be "50 ways to leave your lover," but there are three main ways we interact with customers. While there are many venues of service, I will operate under the assumption you primarily address your customers in one of three ways: face-to-face, telephone, or e-mail. The next few sections tackle these encounters and include practical tips for stellar service. If you do not already think I am crazy, some of my coming suggestions may clinch it. Feel free to disagree with any ideas you are about to read. Perhaps they will be good fodder for water cooler conversations with co-workers. I can hear it now:

"Can you believe what that book said about...?"
"Yeah! No way I'm doing that. I sure hope our principal didn't read it."

Go ahead. Debate it. In fact, roll up the sleeves and engage in a good, old-fashioned hockey brouhaha (I've always wanted to use that word in a written document). I love it. I think it will be a healthy conversation.

Before we jump in to these three modes of service, I think it would be a great time for us to address an important component of our communication: TONE. Research says tone accounts for 38% of all face-to-face communication and 86% of all phone communication.

So, what makes up our tone? Glad you asked. I am about to list five components of tone, and you will recognize distinct similarities to music theory. Please understand none of the components I am about to share are positive or negative. Rather, they carry a neutral value and are simply tools for you to use – like an axe (catch the six-string reference?).

An ax is a great thing if you use it to chop wood. However, it is a terrible thing if you use it to bonk someone on the noggin. The components of tone are similar in that they are neither good nor bad, but can be used to your advantage or disadvantage. The good customer service representative knows how and when to use them.

1. **Tempo.** My wife, a native North Carolinian, likes to remind me, a native New Yorker, that I am in the South now, and I need to stop with the fast talk. Apparently, there is plenty of time for me to make my point, and therefore I need not rush my words.

Obviously, if I am working with a customer lacking English proficiency, then I would be wise to slow down my pace. On the other hand, if I am dealing with "Looney Lisa", who seems to stumble upon a new crisis in her child's classroom every week, I might choose to speak slightly faster, thus giving her the impression my plan (whatever it may be this week) has been tested and proven successful. The situation is under control, and she can trust me.

2. **Volume.** You have probably heard it said, "Never raise your voice to a customer!" But I am here to tell you there may be times when it is appropriate to increase your volume ever so slightly. When "Furious Frank" comes stomping in demanding to see whoever is in charge, he is likely to be loud. At that point, I lower the volume of my voice. Each time he speaks, I respond with a gentler tone. Before long, his speech will fade into a decibel level much more conducive to the realm of logic mentioned earlier. However, when "Whiney Wanda" comes in, I may actually raise my volume just a smidgen (I'll bet you've never seen that word in writing before, have you?). She is always a victim and brings with her the expectation that my school will naturally disappoint her with yet another in a series of failures. My slightly louder tone can serve to convey confidence and let Wanda know I am going to be her advocate.

3. **Range.** You have never heard a song without a chord change, so please do not talk in a robotic monotone. Even if you have just answered the same question 75 times in a row ("It's snowing. Are you closing school early?"), you must sound just as happy to speak with caller number 76. Apply range and inflection to your conversational communication.

4. **Crescendo.** We used to have a football coach at one of the universities in North Carolina without much voice left. I guess those decades of coaching just caused him to lose it. But he never lost his intensity. His interviews were enjoyable to me, because every time I heard him speak I wanted to run through fire for this guy – and his team was the primary rival of my team (Go 'Heels!). He spoke with such passion one could not help but support his cause.

Can we not use the same passion when we describe our school or district? Of course we can. We need to tell the world – with passion – about the wonderful teaching and learning going on in our classrooms. If your tone is lukewarm, then perhaps it would be better if you do not tell the story of your school's wonderfulness. Leave it for someone that can bring it with intensity – like the aforementioned coach.

    Keep in mind there may be times when intensity is not the proper recipe for excellent customer service. Use good judgment.

5. **Key.** Just like the attitude of a song can be conveyed by a major or minor key, I believe we can usually tell when the person on the other end of the phone is smiling. Would you agree? Although I cannot see him, I know if he is smiling by the tone of his voice. Perhaps the muscles in the face change the tone when smiling. I am not sure, but I know this: I believe it so much I bought little mirrors at the flea market for each of my staff members that fit onto our computer monitors. Now we can see what we look like when speaking with callers. If we look grumpy, we probably sound that way, too. Never discount the value of attitude to tone. In one of the most profound lyrical lines in Rock 'n Roll history, Anthrax nailed it: "Change an attitude like you'd change your shorts."

Now that we have explored tone and its components, let's delve into our three genres of service:

- **Face-to-face**
- **Telephone**
- **E-mail**

Face-to-Face

It's in your eyes
The love you hide away
You can't disguise
The things you feel, the thing you say

<u>It's In Your Eyes</u> – Phil Collins

Have you seen your favorite rock star being interviewed live on television? Having to be quick on your feet to answer the often bizarre questions of Suzie Reporter can be quite intimidating. Research indicates face-to-face communication includes three components:

Words	7%
Tone	38%
Gestures	55%

Walk-in visitors are the scariest customers of all. Unlike the phone customers, there is no little orange button with which to put them on hold or even disconnect them. When a customer is standing at my desk, I am expected to come up with some type of answer or solution. The pressure is mounting, and I have to think of something mildly intelligent to say or do – and quickly. When I hire a new customer service representative, I never assign her to work the front counter until she has become familiar with our procedures, information and expectations. Once she has become somewhat comfortable with knowing where to find the information – notice I didn't say she had to know it – then it is time to share her smile with the world.

Good manners and bad breath get you nowhere
<u>New Lace Sleeves</u> – Elvis Costello

Below are six simple steps for serving customers in a face-to-face encounter.

Greet Them

I realize this sounds pretty basic, but I cannot count how many schools I have visited in which I have not been greeted, or I have been greeted after a lengthy wait. The longer I wait the more awkward it gets, and the more my frustration boils. Like Kansas, I soon reach my point of no return.

I recently went house shopping on a Sunday afternoon. My wife was busy, so I took our two kids. We visited a neighborhood in which new houses were being constructed to the specifications of the buyers. We entered the model home and went to the sales office. Once inside this little room, we noticed the agent working with a young couple. Now, I realize sales are his bread and butter, and this may have been a hot customer. However, he never took the time to simply greet my family. Can you imagine being in a small room with us and not even acknowledging our presence? Imagine that scenario for five minutes. It might seem like an eternity. After ten minutes and still no greeting, my children began moving the little homes around on the model neighborhood design. I was fine with it. I thought maybe he would say hello. After fifteen minutes we left – frustrated!

Neil Young must have stumbled across this inept sales guy. I'm sure he was the inspiration for Old Man, "Doesn't mean that much to me to mean that much to you."

Perhaps he didn't need our sale. Maybe he already met his quota. I don't know and don't really care. My home is the biggest purchase of my life. I do know this much, if I'm the boss, we would have a short and not-so-sweet meeting to put an end to this nonsense. All he needed to say is, "Hi. Feel free to look around. I'll be with you shortly." That's all it would have taken for me to feel welcome and to wait patiently. But without the greeting, I felt unwanted and, frankly, in the way.

Smile

You will set the tone for your conversation with your smile. As mentioned earlier, gestures are the single greatest element in communicating with a visitor. No gesture is more universally powerful than the smile. The smile tells the visitor you are not only willing, but privileged, to share your time. The skilled customer service representative can even smile while delivering news the visitor does not want to hear. Hall & Oates put off an inevitable break up by begging, "Sara, smile awhile for me."

Above all, remember, if you refuse to share a smile with the parent, who (in his right mind) would expect you to smile at the children?

Stand Up

I like to think I have exceptionally good manners while my kids just think I'm played out. However, unlike my kids, if you come to visit my home, I will not sit on my couch and yell, "The door's open!"

No, I will get up and go to the door. There I will likely greet you with a hug or handshake. I will invite you inside, and once you are seated, then, and only then, will I sit, too. In the same light, I have instructed my staff to stand whenever a visitor enters The Welcome Center. They are to stand as long as the visitor stands. Once the visitor has been invited to sit, then it is appropriate for the customer service representative to sit also.

Some like to argue this will cause them to sit, stand, sit, stand all day! Probably true. But is that a bad thing? The habit is a good one, and if we're honest, many of us really need the exercise. "Did ya ever think that we would pay the price for being lazy?" asked The Kinks in Did Ya.

Escort

In the world of school customer service, "escort" does not mean what it means in the world of rock. When you are ready to leave my house, I don't sit on the couch and merely say, "Bye." Nope. Instead, I walk you to the door or even out to your car. That's just simple courtesy.

I challenge you to treat your customers likewise. Don't get me wrong. I'm not asking you to escort everyone around your campus or out to the parking lot. Remember we said earlier we were not trying to *send* our customers to solutions, but we want to *take* them to solutions? Well, this is part of the paradigm shift. The old adage about getting to know someone by walking a mile in their moccasins is applicable to the practice of escorting your customers.

I realize it is not always feasible. And I am not asking you to sacrifice the service you would otherwise provide the next customer. But in the rare case you don't have a caller on hold or a line of visitors, then take the four or five steps from your desk to your office door with your guest. Most front offices are rather small. It is not a far journey and doesn't require much time. I have tried to make this my personal habit in an effort to become the "agent" for my Welcome Center visitors. I truly believe there is something symbolic about walking alongside someone – particularly when you have something they need (information, advice, etc.). This powerful gesture creates a bond that says to the customer, "I am here for you." Make the declaration of Johnny Cash, "Because you're mine I walk the line."

Eliminate Barriers

The Who tells us, "We won't get fooled again." Perhaps they were referring to our mixed-up, universal, ingrained notion that desks and counters are supposed to occupy space between the service representative and the customer. Throw that idea out the window.

Before going too far down the road to hypocrisy, I should confess to the two large counters in our Welcome Center. They are a natural barrier to communication with walk-in guests. When I sit behind a desk or stand behind a counter, I am sending a very clear message to my customer: "My place is over here, and your place is over there." Guess which place has all the information? Guess which place is more likely decorated and comfortable? That's right, not he customers' place.

To combat this problem (and I chose the word "problem" on purpose), I am trying to make a habit of standing off to the side of the counter when working with a customer. Please understand, I dread being around the type of guy Seinfeld rightfully labels the "close talker." He freaks me out, and I don't want to be that guy. So I do maintain a healthy distance. In fact, if I can smell your breath, that's much too close for me.

Standing to the side of the counter is a subtle way to do away with turf discrepancies. Your office may not have the capacity to try this, or least not as currently designed. If your desk creates a barrier, maybe you can angle it so customers will naturally stand at the side of your desk instead of in front of your desk.

Send Them with a Souvenir

In <u>Modern Woman</u>, Billy Joel sang, *"What if she figures out you're not very smart?"* Well, if you arm yourself with great resources, then you don't have to be smart.

I am continually disappointed by the number of schools I visit that fail to keep printed information on hand in the front office. Yes, kids, I am into electronic communications. However, every frontliner should have a brochure within reach to describe the wonderful attributes of the school. They are easy to produce and cheap to copy. There are many software programs for creating them so you needn't spend money. On the other hand, don't hand out cheesy looking flyers. Make them look professional and convey the appearance of a school that has its act together. Maybe you could run a contest with a prize for the student that creates the best brochure. Be sure your printed material is aligned with the standards of your school district. Everything should include the school system's logo and tag line if appropriate. If you have questions, it is never a bad idea to run your brochures by the district's Director of Communications.

In addition to brochures, make sure all front office staff members have their own business cards. They are very inexpensive. In fact, many school districts have their own print shops which render the cards even more cost-effective. Sticking with the "frontliner as an advocate" motif, how wonderful for a customer to walk away with a business card listing the name and contact information for the person with whom he just met. In our Welcome Center, we have a card holder for each representative right on the front counter. That way, whichever one of us happens to be assisting a customer can easily grab our card and put it in the visitor's hand as a way to both thank and invite further conversations. "Take my card with you and don't hesitate to give me a shout if you think of any more questions."

No matter the strategies you choose to employ, make every attempt to create a physical environment conducive to "take" versus "send" relationships with your walk-in customers. Keep in mind, while these are the most nerve-racking encounters for a customer service representative – they are also intimidating for the customer. This is the most pressure-filled type of conversation and has the most potential for eruption. But, it also has the most potential for establishing or recovering positive, significant, long-term relationships. A frontliner smooth in face-to-face interactions can be a principal's best friend. The tone set in the front office can resonate throughout the entire campus. It may seem corny, but practicing these and other strategies is a great use of time and energy. Finding a combination that works for you can change your entire professional outlook and make you seemingly indispensable!

Telephone

Operator, can you help me place this call?

Operator – Jim Croce

Rock stars rarely have to deal with the intrusion of telephone calls, after all, that's what agents and managers are for! Alas, for us commoners, telephones are an every day reality. Though I can envision it happening in the near future, I have yet to see a school secretary utilizing an iChat or other camera phone to interact with telephone customers. Thus, we can agree with the research that claims our telephone communication falls into two categories:

| Tone | 86% |
| Words | 14% |

Unlike the face-to-face conversations, we do not have to worry about the intimidation factor. Nor do we have the luxury of the gestures. Instead, we must pay extra special attention to the tone we use. It is important to note how quick the caller will make a judgment about you and your school. It may be as quick as your initial greeting!

Are you **prepared** to do all the **work necessary** to recover a customer's opinion based upon a bogus greeting? Well, you shouldn't have to. Yoo hoo, McFly? Simply implement a high-quality four-part greeting to every call, and you will create the conditions for a wonderful phone conversation. Be sure every person in your school or district answers the same way. It must be consistent.

You guessed it. Here come the four parts.

Four-Part Greeting

1.   The Smiling Foreword

Just like in the beginning of this book, the foreword is not designed to offer new information. Does that make it worthless? No. Quite the contrary. A well-written foreword (Thanks, Tom!) can set the stage for a great book. And a friendly tone in the first few words can set the stage for a great interaction. For rockers, the first song of the set establishes the energy level for the whole concert.

You see, the words you choose for your telephone foreword don't matter much to me. You can start with "Hello", "Good morning" or even "Happy Thursday". The caller will likely not hear or not pay attention to your greeting. He will, however, notice your tone. Hence, the *smiling* foreword.

The important thing to remember is the welcoming attitude you convey in the initial uttering of your voice. Just as the tone of a singer's voice can clue you into the kind of music to which you are listening: soft and smooth Jazz; twangy and nasal Country & Western; screaming Death Metal; tone matters. Not only will the tone of your foreword tell the customer your expectations for the conversation, but a smile will also put you in the best frame of mind to bring patience and tolerance to the interaction.

2. Your Name

Shakespeare postulated that "a rose by any other name would still smell as sweet," but getting a frontliner to add her name is a surprisingly controversial inclusion to the greeting. I recently consulted with a school district in the Midwest and was puzzled as to why personnel at all of their schools were using a similar greeting, but with only three parts. They were withholding their names from the customers. Later I learned the local employee union frowned on the practice. I really had to think about that one. I suppose you could build a case for never giving your real name to anyone for any reason. Seems a little over-the-top to me. Maybe that's why they created stage names. Talk about "paranoia the destroyer."

Personally, I like knowing the name of the person with whom I am speaking. I think there are very distinct advantages for providing your name. First, it removes another barrier. It marks the initiation of the "frontliner as advocate" relationship. I have found customers seem to enjoy, and even feel somewhat de-pressurized, when I give them my name (if asked nicely, I might even throw in an autograph).

Next, offering my name can minimize confusion. This is especially true when multiple people or departments get involved in assisting a customer. Often, I find myself speaking with customers who have already been given some information by a colleague from another department. If I just knew the name of the person with whom the customer spoke, I could easily track down an answer. Without the name,

I have to go back to the very beginning of the story. This unnecessarily consumes mass quantities (Conehead reference) of precious time and is wicked (for you New Englanders) frustrating for me and the customer.

Finally, offering your name to the customer provides a measure of accountability. Knowing the customer has my name, I am naturally going to try a little harder for my service to be memorable – in the good way. We'll talk more about accountability in the Revival chapter to follow.

If giving your name is a problem, then simply make up a name. Just make sure all your co-workers are clued in. I would hate for a customer to ask for Phil, the guy they spoke with earlier in the day, only to be told there is no such person.

Wanna have some fun? Call a few schools in your area. If the frontliner does not offer a name, ask for one. You might try, "With whom am I speaking?" Sometimes you get an immediate answer, almost apologetic in nature. "Oh, sorry, this is Debbie. How can I help you?" But other times you sense just how annoyed the representative is by your question, and you get an entirely different answer. "THIS IS MRS. JONES."

I notice myself becoming more and more crotchety in my old age. I have made it a habit to ask for a name just as a silly amusement for my dull little mind. Or maybe I'm using passive aggression in an attempt to prove a point to a frontliner who is much too agitated to ever pick up on my cowardly subtleties. Either way, I plan to continue asking for a name. It is a good practice, and I encourage you to do the same.

Like Lynyrd Skynyrd, I just want to know, "What's your name?" Maybe one day everyone will offer their name when picking up the phone, and our planet will finally be safe.

3. Your School or Department

> "Good evening folks, we're [insert band name here],
> and it's great to be in [your town's name]!"

Rock stars make it a point to let you know who and where they are. It is always good to confirm the name of your organization, but even more so when you are a school district representative. Schools and administrative offices contain many, many phones. Frequently, our customers get bounced from person to person looking for assistance. I'm sure you have had plenty of customers immediately ask, "So, which department are you in?," "What school is this?" or even "And why am I speaking with you?"

Go ahead and give them this information up front, so they can get right to their question feeling satisfied they have reached the right department. And think about this: what if the customer just starts in on you with a long story about her situation, only to find out you are not the appropriate one to assist with her specific question. She will need to be transferred to someone else. What a waste of time for both of you. Eliminate that problem by simply stating the name of your school or department. It is a good habit. And by the way, you can offer your name and department in either order, just as long as both are part of your greeting.

4. Submission

The final component of the four-part greeting is simply your offer of service. You humbly submit to the request of the caller. "How can I help you?", "How can I be of service?" and "What can I do for you today?" are all acceptable. Remember, it is the tone rather than the words that will impact your caller.

The nicest submission I ever heard was from the least likely place. I once had to make a call about my hot water heater and expected to hear (in a disinterested tone), "Yo. Lou here."

Instead, I heard what sounded like the voice of an angel on the other end of the phone. Her four-part greeting was perfect and, though I could not see her, she definitely sounded as if she was smiling. While I never met her face-to-face, I was convinced she looked like a supermodel. Perhaps that's where Debbie Harry now spends her time (hey, at 63 she's still a knockout). Why? Simply because of the way she answered the phone. It was beautiful.

The most memorable part of her greeting was the submission. I must warn you, it is not for the feint of heart. Here goes: **"How can I make you smile today?"**

Wow! I dropped the phone and remained speechless for weeks (which is quite a feat for those who know me well!). Similar to Simon and Garfunkel, I too had a vision softly creeping that left its seeds while I was sleeping.

I teach this stuff for a living, and I have never heard anything so inviting (and yes, I already know what you are thinking, but go along with me on this).

Well, I rushed into the office and gathered my team together to share with them my new idea for tweaking our four-part greeting. I could see the look in their eyes. "Awww. Here we go again. Nash has been reading another book."

But we did it anyhow – against their better judgment.

I would be lying if I said it was successful, but it certainly made for an interesting day. So, I would like to issue another challenge (oh no, he wouldn't). Next time you are at your last day of work prior to a long vacation, and you are in such a state of euphoria that nobody can ruin your day, try using the same submission to conclude your four-part greeting. Try it with twenty calls in a row. Just see what happens. I realize it is not easy, but try to have fun with it. You must be in a great mood though. You can't say "How can I make you smile today?" without being really happy and moderately animated.

What should you expect? Well, a variety of answers. Some callers will think you are nuts. Some will just be annoyed. Others will give you sarcastic responses in an attempt to be funny. Expect a few perverts to chime in with their own ideas. But most of all, expect hesitation. We found the callers to be taken aback by the killer kindness.

Again, I don't recommend, "How can I make you smile today?" as your regular submission. But just for fun, take it out for a test drive and then shoot me an e-mail describing your experiences. Should be fun.

> "Good morning. This is Jeff in the Welcome Center.
>
> How can I help you?"

The four-part greeting should be implemented by all school district personnel and volunteers. It needs to be the way business gets done. I have had multiple discussions over the years with colleagues who claim the four-part greeting takes too long to say and is wasteful of the customer's time. I beg to differ. I can say "Good morning. This is Jeff in The Welcome Center, how can I help you?" in about 1.8 seconds without rushing through it. That is much shorter than having to be asked "Who is this?", "What is your name?" or "Which school is this?"

Getting asked any of those questions and supplying an answer can take you up to ten or even fifteen seconds. It's much quicker and more professional to make it part of your standard greeting. It is also very easy to implement. Like much else we do, it is simply a matter of making it our habit. Answer your next twenty calls with a four-part greeting, and it will become your habit. Say it slow and clear. It should flow smoothly out of your mouth, across the telephone lines and into your caller's ear – just like Sade's "smooth operator."

One last tidbit about the four-part greeting, technology is available to assist in answering the phones. On my computer-based phone system, I can record my greeting any way I want it to sound. In fact, I can have many pre-recorded greetings starting with, "Good morning…", "Good afternoon…" or even "Happy St. Patrick's Day…". The program will hold more greetings than I care to record. I can then select the one I want to use and every call that comes in will be answered with my pre-recorded greeting. The caller hears it and thinks I am talking to him. Once the caller responds, then I jump in to engage in a conversation. I really don't bother to use that feature very often, but it is available and it allows me to sound just as perky at 4:30 in the afternoon as I might at 8:30 in the morning. That's me – perky!

Voicemail Abuse

I am of the opinion that voicemail is the single most abused form of technology in schools and districts nationwide. It is a wonderful tool, and the inventor should be given an award. Not the Grammy, of course, but maybe the Nobel. Do customers get frustrated when they look up a phone number and place the call only to hear a machine on the other end of the phone? Of course. We all do. But we can take steps to alleviate their angst and encourage them to utilize the technology. Let's look at a few ways to improve the actual message they might hear when they call you.

Quit Your Yappin'

You talk too much / You worry me to death
You talk too much / You even worry my pet
You just talk – talk too much
<u>You Talk Too Much</u> – Joe Jones

Every great Rock 'n Roll song is memorable – that's what makes it great. But it doesn't have to say much to touch a cord with people. Like Paula Abdul, your message should be short and sweet (oh, come on!). The biggest problem I see with voicemail messages is the length. People talk way too much. My voicemail system, like probably many of yours, has a built-in option for the caller to hit the # sign and go straight to the beep so she can leave a message. Unfortunately, many of my callers don't know about that feature, so they are obligated to listen to my entire message before they hear the beep and can leave a message of their own. So, out of respect for your customers' time, please find ways to reduce the amount of patience required before they can speak. I strongly suggest writing out your message prior to recording. Look for excess verbiage. I'll bet there are some things in your message right now that can be deleted. Some song writers agonize over just the right phrasing or rhythm. While this is probably not necessary, do take the time to do it right.

The most common unnecessary phrase heard in way too many voicemail messages is, "I'm not here right now." or "I can't come to the phone right now."

Naturally, I figured that one out. Thanks for telling me, Captain Obvious. If you are reading this and know you have a similar phrase in your message, please make a note to self to change it immediately upon completion of this chapter.

The next most common mistake is the inclusion of, "after the beep." Maybe (probably not, but maybe) for the first few years in voicemail history, back in the day when it was just catching on, it would have been necessary to instruct the caller to wait for the beep. However, I would suggest those days are gone. You can officially retire that phrase. This generation of callers knows they cannot simply speak over your message. They know to wait…they just don't want to wait long. And they shouldn't have to.

Avoid the Play-By-Play

Please do the whole world a favor and avoid the rundown of every event on your schedule. Good grief, Charlie Brown!

"Good morning. This is Mary. As much as I really, really want to hear from you, I am unable to come to my phone right now. After eating a healthy breakfast I will be meeting with the leadership team from 9:00 until 11:00. Then I will head over to Presley Elementary for 45 minutes before my 12:00 lunch meeting with the Chamber of Commerce. I will be with the Superintendent from 2:30 until 3:30 and then leaving early to take precious Suzie to her piano lesson. Your message is really, really important to me, and I have every hope of calling you back some day so please leave your name, phone number, title, zip code, employee id number and a minimum of three e-mail addresses – after the beep."

Yes, I realize the above is an exaggeration, but probably not by too much for some of the messages I have heard. You truly needn't let us know everything you have planned for the day. If you really feel compelled to tell us something about your schedule, then simply tell us when you will be returning messages. Again, the caller doesn't care where you are or how important you consider yourself. You do not need to justify your reason for being away from the phone.

Real-Time Messages

Using a real-time message, one that is changed daily and likely begins with "Good morning. Today is Tuesday, October…", is great – but only if you are completely anal about updating it EVERY SINGLE MORNING. To skip an update would be a customer service crime. In fact, if I call your number and hear a voicemail recording that is from a previous day (or week, in some cases), I am much less likely to leave you a message. Why? I figure if you haven't bothered to even update your recording, then surely you won't bother to return calls.

Harsh, I know. But don't lose sight of the point. While real-time messages can be more useful than generic messages if implemented properly, they also require more work and have the potential to cause bigger problems. Personally, I choose to utilize a generic message. I only change it if I am going to be out of the office and unable to return calls for more than 24 hours. And even then, I avoid lengthy descriptions of my whereabouts. I do, however, like to offer other avenues for assistance – particularly for emergency situations – "if you need immediate help, please call…."

Be sure, also, you know how to change your message from the road if that capability exists. Keep the directions with you just in case an emergency springs up. You never know when you are going to get called out of town or be sick in bed for a week. The last thing you want to do is travel all the way to your office just to change the voicemail recording.

Mention All Recipients

The lesson of this section has come with a price. I have taken many beatings because someone else's voicemail fails to contain the names of all possible recipients (yes, I am a victim). I'll bet many of you can feel my pain. Let me share a hypothetical example.

Dr. Williams, the Director of Human Resources, has his phones forwarded to his receptionist, Veronica, because he is on yet another vacation. A customer calls in to the main number and asks for Dr. Williams. I transfer the call to him, but it goes to Veronica's desk. Unfortunately, Veronica is still enjoying her three-hour siesta (after all, while the cat's away…). The caller knows none of this, but only hears the voicemail of someone other than Dr. Williams. So what will the caller do? You guessed it. Call me back, and let me have it for transferring her to the wrong number!

Sure, voicemail can be a wonderful tool. Just use it properly. Be on the lookout for good or not-so-good messages. When you hear a message that doesn't sound quite right – for any reason – ask yourself if your current message contains similarly annoying components. On the contrary, when you hear a message that strikes you as endearing, figure out what you like about it and give consideration as to how you can emulate certain aspects.

Above all, keep the tone of your message pleasant. Don't get too wrapped up in yourself to sound friendly. Never give the impression of sounding more efficient and professional than warm and welcoming. After all, the whole point of having voicemail is to communicate with the caller. Your message should not be intimidating.

Are you smiling when you record it?

Email

Write me a letter
Write me a letter
Write it today
I'm goin' away

<u>Write Me A Letter</u> – Aerosmith

A few years back, our Office of Communications decided to add a feature to the school district website that allows viewers to send e-mail to the district in general. We figured responding to these messages will certainly add to someone's workload, but whom? As you probably guessed, they were directed to the Welcome Center. In hindsight, I would have it no other way.

I erroneously assumed the messages sent via e-mail would be similar to the questions sent via phone and visitor. Wow, was I wrong! Those jokers staying up all hours of the night, downing java (like it was coffee) and blasting my school district are much bolder than any other variety of customer I serve. The cusswords are eye-popping. Some of them could make Frank Zappa blush! My vocabulary expanded quicker than my belly at a buffet! In fact, I am convinced some writers go so far as to create a free e-mail account on Yahoo or Hotmail simply to blindside me with a scalding message about reassignment, weather cancellations or some other hot tamale. Call me skittish, but when I try to respond, I often find the messages bouncing back to me as if they have already cancelled those accounts.

Most of the tips I would offer regarding proper e-mail utilization are common sense, and you likely have heard them before, but let me emphasize this one important piece of unwanted advice with as much compassion as I can muster:

DON'T SCREW IT UP!!!

In just the past ten years, more people have been humiliated, brow-beaten, disciplined or fired due to poor e-mail judgment than I would know how to count. It's not that they don't know how to send or retrieve an e-mail message…it's just sometimes people forget to think. So allow me to point out a few important reminders for answering customer e-mail.

Use Customer Name When Possible

"Say my name, say my name" is a famous plea from Destiny's Child and a good place to start. As a rule of thumb, I avoid the use of "Dear" in my greeting. Instead I simply insert the name the customer provided on his original message. If he signed it Mr. Smith, then I will greet him likewise. If he signed it Tim Johnson, then I will usually use Tim. In fact, being that e-mail is still considered slightly less formal than a letter, I prefer to address e-mail customers by first name. The only time I will use Mr. Johnson is when I am quite sure it is a hot-button issue that will likely be escalated and forwarded to many others.

Unfortunately, many e-mail communications I receive don't include any name. In those cases, I do not apply a greeting to my response. It is important you don't assume the customer's name. When no name is given, it is tempting to look at the sender's e-mail address and decipher cindyjones@xyz.com is named Cindy. But that is quite a stretch. It may be Cindy's husband, child or friend sending the message instead.

Begin By Thanking

Thanks to you it will be done / For you to me are the only one
Thank You – Led Zeppelin

All e-mail responses should begin with a thank you. Don't make it flowery or patronizing. Something as simple as, "Good morning and thank you for writing" will do just fine. Show your appreciation and let that be enough.

End With Invitation

Call me on the line
Call me, call me any anytime
Call Me – Blondie

Just like your face-to-face and phone conversations, your e-mail response should end with an invitation for future conversation. Again, keep it simple but sincere. In recent years, I have been using "Feel free to call or write if I can serve you in any other way."

Forwarding

Sitting here in limbo / Waiting for the tide to flow
Sitting here in limbo / Knowing that I have to go
<u>Sitting In Limbo</u> – Jimmy Cliff

Likely, many of the e-mail correspondence you receive need to be forwarded to a principal, director, superintendent or other colleague. I am always tempted to merely forward the message and move on to the next one. However, doing so assumes great customer service risk. If the person I am forwarding the message to fails to respond, then it will appear to the customer as if his message was not addressed at all. Therefore, I like to send two messages: one as a reply to the sender; and one as a forward to the person I deem best able to assist the writer. To the *sender* I write something along these lines:

> "Good afternoon and thank you for writing. To get the best answer to your question, I am forwarding your message to Mr. Dave Krause, our school district's Director of Special Education Services. You can follow up, if needed, by contacting him at dkrause@school.com or by phone at 555-555-5555. Please feel free to call or write if I can serve you in any other way."

To the *co-worker* receiving my forward, I might send something similar to the following:

> "Good afternoon. I hope this note finds you well! The message below arrived via our district website. Please cc me on your response to the sender. Thanks and enjoy the rest of your day."

You will notice I did not give them the option of not responding. I also did not ask for the information so I can respond on their behalf. I might do this if I was the secretary to this person, but not for colleagues in other departments or schools. I want the customer to hear back from the "expert" without any possibility of me misinterpreting or miscommunicating information.

I will ask to be included on the cc for two reasons. First, and most importantly, I want to be sure the sender receives a response. Second, I ask to be included for my own edification. If I can learn the answer to the question, then perhaps I can answer it next time without needing to forward the message.

I must warn you, when you ask to be included as a cc you may see some things…scary things! To start with, I don't receive many cc responses. That tells me the principal/director either is not responding at all or does not want me to see what is being sent. Both scenarios are serious red flags. And when I do get cc'd, I am often ashamed of the spelling/syntax/grammar being sent out from some of the school district's highest ranking staff!

This brings us to the next point.

Proofread

Natural reflex
Pendulum swing
You might be too dizzy
To do the right thing
Stick It Out – Rush

I realize e-mail is less formal and therefore more susceptible to "I-M" language (if you don't know, ask your middle schooler). And in a business setting, that may be absolutely fine. However, in an institution of learning and teaching, ***mistakes are unacceptable***. I can hear them squawking at the tennis club, "I can't believe they want us to pass this bond. They can't even send out a note without errors."

Don't ever let the error-filled e-mail message be one with your name attached. Be sure to proofread for technical errors, but also for errors of tone. I'll bet we have all responded to an e-mail in a way that was found to be offensive – even when we meant no ill will. Because e-mail communication consists entirely of words, without the luxury of gestures or tone, it is easily misconstrued. I will frequently ask a co-worker to read over an e-mail before I send it simply to make sure it doesn't come off as abrasive.

> *Don't you say a word unless you're pretty sure that you want it analyzed*
> <u>A Slow Descent</u> – Straylight Run

Another strategy I often implement is to write my response and then, before I send it, take a five-minute break. Get up, go to the restroom, get a drink of water, talk with a co-worker about this week's *American Idol* performances and then come back and re-read my outgoing message. Remarkably, I will end up making changes to the message nearly half the time. I sometimes amaze myself with the things I *almost* sent.

If that had gone out…

Contact Information

> *Who needs information*
> *This high off the ground?*
> *Just give me confirmation*
> *We could win a million pounds*
> <u>Who Needs Information?</u> – Roger Waters

Don't be one of those. You know who I mean. Those who guard contact information as if it was sacred. Puh-leeze. Spare me. Include all of your contact information as part of your autosignature. Just because you are responding to an e-mail does not mean you should avoid giving out your phone number.

To be proper, you should have your name, title, department or school, school district, physical address, phone number, fax number and e-mail address at the bottom of all outgoing e-mail messages.

The biggest mistake I see is folks forgetting to include their e-mail address along with their other information. I guess we might assume since the outgoing response is being sent via e-mail the receiver will automatically know our address. Not so fast. Be a good egg and include it with your other contact information.

Save

Just like you never want to be the only guy to show up at a gunfight with a knife, you also don't want to be called to account for an e-mail conversation in which you have no record of the incoming or outgoing messages. I always want to be the most prepared participant at any meeting in which I am in attendance. The ability to record and keep correspondence is a wonderful attribute of e-mail. Don't let a lack of record-keeping come back to bite you.

Furthermore, beware of e-mail systems that trash messages stored longer than 90 days (or whatever length is programmed) in online folders. I would strongly suggest using an offline folder. If you are not sure about your e-mail system, check with your technology department.

Newspaper Test

Extra! Extra! Read all about it!
The Pinball Wizard and the Miracle Cure
Miracle Cure – The Who

Finally, if you have second thoughts about the appropriateness of content in any of your e-mail conversations, here's your litmus test: Would you want to read that content in tomorrow's newspaper with your name attributed to it? If not, then it might be best to stay away from such subjective content. Keep in mind, this goes for both your incoming and outgoing messages.

As public employees (and yes your salary is paid by the community as they love to remind you), all of your written and typed messages are public records. At any time, a reporter, or anyone else for that matter, can complete a public records request and ask/demand to see all of your incoming and outgoing e-mail correspondence. We have no choice but to provide it. You can see the potential for huge portions of embarrassment for both you and your employer. Be careful with the jokes, rumors, political conversations and discussions of people in and out of your school.

Accurate & Appropriate – Gotta Have Both

> *Hey, I know that it's hard for you*
> *To say the things that we both know are true*
> <u>I Keep Forgetting</u> – Michael McDonald

Allow me to expound on the difference between an accurate e-mail and an appropriate e-mail. **Your message really needs to be both accurate and appropriate**. For instance, if you receive a message asking what time your building opens, it could be accurate to respond with "8:30." But that would not be appropriate. The appropriate response would be:

> "Good morning and thank you for writing. Our building opens at 8:30 am. Please feel free to call or write if I can ever be of additional service."

I know, I know. Writing that much is time-consuming. Fortunately, somebody invented "copy" and "paste." You can simply paste in your thank you sentence and your offer of additional service. Better yet, you can be more like me (wish everyone was) and have the thank you sentence and the offer to serve saved as part of your autosignature. Thus, you only need to type "Our building opens at 8:30 am." You will then have a perfectly written, fool-proof response which is both accurate and appropriate – and will require minimal time.

Stalkers & Critics: Difficult Customers

No you don't
Have to treat me like a fool
No you don't
Have to be so bloody cool
No you don't
Have to make up all the rules
No you don't

<u>No You Don't</u> – Pat Benatar

When you're a rock star, you have a fabulous world of hit records, adoring fans and praise from <u>Rolling Stone</u> magazine. However, there is a dark side to the fame. Those of us in the world of customer service understand that dark side all too well. Although our challengers don't have the official title of "critic," we've still got plenty of 'em! Fickle fans? I bet you can name quite a few. You may even have your fair share of stalkers: no names, please.

In my customer service training classes, I give my favorite types of customers fictitious names: Veronica Victim, Outraged Oscar, Whacked-out Wendy, Haughty Henry and Political Polly just to name a few. And, no, they are not named after any of my former customers (fingers crossed behind back).

Obviously, the name of each "fictional" customer tells us something about the character of that customer-type. Personalizing the customers can evoke memories of similar experiences as well as prepare us for future encounters. There are more types of customers than I care to name, but I like to emphasize ad nauseam the need to customize your service habits. **Building, maintaining and restoring customer relationships is not a one-size-fits-all endeavor.**

In one of my favorite training exercises, I split the class into groups. Each group is given an in-depth description of one of the customers named above. The group is charged with producing a list of strategies for working with that particular customer. The group reports its findings to the rest of the class which is invited to add any additional thoughts or ideas. This typically leads to hilarious conversations regarding outrageous customers of years gone by. Recently, one participant gave us a dissertation on a specific customer-type after pronouncing her expertise in this area – she claimed Haughty Henry was her ex-husband!

Are there any strategies applicable to all customers? Sure. Take a look at the list below.

Listen

I should know better
But I never really listen to me
<u>Listen</u> – Far Too Jones

Customers want to be heard. However, customer service representatives know a lot of answers, especially if they have been in their position for a while. On numerous occasions, I have caught myself committing a terrible customer service snafu. In fact, if I search deep within, I must admit I possess a terrible customer service habit. You see, and this is just between you and me, I have a tendency to be impatient with callers and visitors who struggle to get their questions out. Yeah, go figure.

I fail to remember the customer's question is new and relevant to him. I may hear the same question multiple times hourly. So when I hear certain key words in a conversation that lead me to believe I know what the customer needs, I blurt out my response before the customer completes his question. Often, I am correct in my assumption of his question, and I provide the right answer. But none of that matters if I don't listen to the customer's entire question before I interject a response. Being correct is nice, but not at the expense of rudeness.

Here's the kicker. Because I recognize my fault in this area, I find myself noticing it in others as well. To bring my hypocrisy to a boil, I now get extremely frustrated when someone begins talking before I can complete my whole sentence or thought. I really don't like being interrupted. How boorish some people can be!

My point is this: as the old adage says, **don't just hear your customers…listen.** It is amazing what you can learn by saying nothing and only listening.

Affirm

Have you ever heard about rock stars that don't want to be in the spotlight? They are committed to the "art" but not to the fame. For them, it's difficult to connect with people they don't know. Neil Peart of Rush sums this feeling up in the song <u>Limelight</u>, *"I can't pretend a stranger is a long awaited friend."* So too, do our customers have anxiety about approaching us, even more so than we have of them. As such, it is good practice for the frontliner to affirm the customer's issue or question as legitimate. This can be a very simple and nonchalant process. If you sense your customer is nervous or unsure about even bringing up his question, complaint or issue, you could say something like, "That's a great question," "You are really doing your homework," "I should know the answer. Let me check for you," or even, "You're asking a very popular question."

When you dig beneath the service, you notice this is really about putting your customer at ease and removing any emotional time bombs that are set to go off right there in your office if all doesn't go exactly as planned. It's like learning the moves to an intricate dance, which **you** are leading.

Customers frequently don't know how to ask their question or how to navigate the school system. Offering verbal assurances is akin to hand-holding and brings a sense of relief to a tense situation.

Be Honest

It is very tempting to make a promise to a difficult customer just to appease her. Committing to give her what she wants just to get her out of your sight can seem like the easy road to sanity. You might think I am talking about the loud, boisterous and potentially violent type. But I am also thinking about the most annoying of all customers – the whiner.

Stay strong! Don't give up the store. You cannot make empty promises. Sooner or later, you or someone else will have to answer for those promises. Songwriters are known for digging deep and connecting with a truth inside, but just as songs can be taken more than one way, so can your words. **Be careful what you say. Beware what they think you say**.

Keep An Open Mind

The Boomtown Rats gave us great advice when they sang, "*Watch out for the normal people.*" I, for one, am prone to discredit certain customers based on their repeat annoyances. However, it is vital the customer service representative maintains an open mind. You just never know when the customer may be right. Though it pains us to consider the notion, at some point the customer may have a legitimate beef! We cannot be so closed off that we instantly rule out any potential credibility or "rightness" the customer may bring. **Watch out for your personal biases.**

Don't Try to Win

I don't know about you, but when it comes to dealing with difficult customers, I have a natural tendency to whole-heartedly buy in to Freddie Mercury's challenge: I will, I will rock you…and then I will be the champion. **Conversations can very quickly become contests**. This goes back to our previous discussion of pet peeves. What is it that primes you for a competitive stance? Does it happen when the customer mentions "you people"? Does it happen when the customer provides his notion of a better idea for handling your business? Or does it happen when the customer insults your school or district?

Either way, getting into a whizzing match with a customer, while it can be a great way to pass the time on an otherwise boring day, is in reality just an exercise in futility with no real good consequences except for the trivial gratification you may get from "putting that joker in his place!" Be sure to consider the cost of such fulfillment.

It's All About Now

> *Yesterday all my troubles seemed so far away*
> *Now it looks as though they're here to stay*
> *Oh I believe in yesterday*
> <u>Yesterday</u> – The Beatles

Difficult customers are notorious for their attempts to pull you back into the past or drag you into the future against your will. Be on the lookout for such attempts. Don't give in, Friend. Stand your ground and **remain in the present**.

How might they draw you out of the present, you ask? Great question. Let's identify a couple key phrases for which to be on guard. First, beware of any conversation that begins with, "Well, you have never…" If you try to defend that accusation, then you are now in a discussion about the past. If the customer lets into you with, "Why should I believe you will ever…" then you should beware of entering a debate about the future.

You can always pull the discussion back to the present by simply asking "How can I address the concern you have today?"

Words/Body/Tone Match

In dealing with difficult customers, of every category, always be cognizant of the messages you are sending. You are probably spending most of your energy selecting just the right words to make your point. However, be sure the **tones** you employ and the **gestures** you intertwine are matching the **words** you have spoken.

For instance, telling Veronica Victim you really want to help her, but looking at her with one eye purposely squinted and the opposite eyebrow raised may send a mixed message. Verbally, you are claiming to "feel her pain," but your non-verbal message tells her, and it may be purely her perception, you think she should be locked up for her own safety!

If your customer determines you are like Foreigner and *"playing head games,"* then you can count on making a difficult situation even worse.

Seek Common Ground

In a business/customer relationship, the business and the customer each bring a different interest to the table, but ones that can be satisfied by the other. What I mean to say is the business wants my money and I want their product. If we both agree on the rules of the deal (price, quality, etc.), then we make an exchange. If however, my check bounces, the business will want their product back. Or if the product is not everything it was advertised to be, then I may demand a refund of my payment. In this sense the business/customer relationship is adversarial. It runs smoothly only when each party gets its interdependent needs met by the other. If ever one feels shafted…look out!

Fortunately, the school/customer relationship is very different. While school customer service representatives are at many disadvantages when compared to business customer service representatives, there is one tremendous advantage owned by school representatives that causes them to look at their business counterparts and sing the infamous words of M.C. Hammer: "You can't touch this!"

The advantage of which I write is the notion of **common ground.** You see, the school customer service representative, whether she realizes it or not (and too many times she does not), has a place of common ground to which she and her customer can simultaneously reside. Instead of entering the relationship with opposite interests, the school representative and the customer bring the same basic desire to the table. When you zoom in, you can clearly see this common ground: **the success of the child** – it trumps all other interests.

Unfortunately, the school representative often comes to believe the parent is not all that interested in the child's success – and sometimes with good reason. On the flip side, it can easily appear to an angry parent that the school representatives are not interested in helping the child.

A skilled school customer service representative will keep the notion of higher ground up her sleeve and bring it out as a reminder whenever necessary. It is totally okay for the parent to hear about the common ground multiple times during any discussion. It should never be spoken in an accusatory way or in a manner that would insinuate the school caring more than the parent (that would lead to bad things, really bad things!).

There are people in your life who've come and gone
They let you down and hurt your pride
Better put it all behind you, life goes on
You keep carrying that anger, it'll eat you up inside
Heart Of The Matter – Don Henley

My World Tour: The Welcome Center

It's the end of the world as we know it
It's the end of the world as we know it
It's the end of the world as we know it and I feel fine

It's The End Of The World As We Know It – R.E.M.

Ten years ago, I was an administrator in our school district's Office of Student Assignment. As you know, student assignment is always a contentious area, but especially in a district that, at the time, was growing by over 5,000 students per year. Yes, that is over 5,000 additional students each school year! We typically open three to seven new schools per year. The problem is…somebody has to attend these schools. Hence, we move many students from existing schools into new schools. And, for example, if School X just lost 400 students to a neighboring new school, then we might move 200 from over-capacity School Y to backfill School X. When all is said and done, we usually reassign between 5,000 and 10,000 students per year. I realize that sounds like a lot of movement, but it is only about 5% of the student population. Of course, if your child is moved, then you have a perceived permission to show your rear end (can you sense my battle scars?).

Reassignment is simply a way of life in my neck of the woods – and in any growing area. According to a band called Garbage, *"The trick is to keep breathing."*

Well, interestingly, between all the threats and bribes from parents in attempts to get their children into the schools of their choice instead of the schools assigned to their addresses, I found myself getting many phone calls entirely unrelated to student assignment. Bizarre stuff would come through my phone line. When I traced the origins of these calls, I found the receptionist of our central office building was sending me this aromatic bouquet of callers.

Knowing this receptionist is the most popular person in our entire school district, and an icon who knows every person and even every phone number, I approached her gently. I was not at all wanting to accuse her of misdirecting calls to me. In fact, I had developed a wonderful friendship with her and recognized her as one of the genuinely kindest and most effective employees on any campus. I was just curious as to why she was sending these callers to my office. Her response completely changed my professional life.

She said the calls were sent to me for two reasons. First, she knew I would answer my phone. Second, she trusted me to be friendly with her customers. WOW!

Upon further analysis, it is slowly starting to make sense. After all these years it is finally coming together (I told you I am a little late on the draw). However, her trust in my ability to serve is both humbling and uplifting. She explained how she was required to handle all of the incoming phone calls, visitors, packages, etc. arriving to the front desk of our building. She did not have time to locate specific information, but also did not want to send a customer to someone who never picks up his phone or to someone who picks up his phone but we wish he didn't. Due to the high volume of customers and her being a staff of one, she had to move the call and get to the next one immediately.

What terrible service (obviously rushed and incomplete) was being provided by such a wonderful service representative! Please understand, this is absolutely no reflection on the efforts of the individual, she is still providing excellent service to this day. Rather it speaks to the former systemic structure of our district office. Oh, and did I mention the central office should be the customer service flagship of any school district? Anyone else see the unfortunate hypocrisy? I have seen the same scenario play out in many districts with which I have consulted. Is your central office the shining star of customer service for your district? Does it set the example for all of the schools in the district?

Anyhow, soon after is when I opened my big mouth. I had an idea – an idea that would change my whole career.

So make the best of this test / And don't ask why
It's not a question / But a lesson learned in time
<u>Good Riddance</u> – Green Day

I was eating lunch with a colleague, and I mentioned the notion that somebody should (SOMEBODY SHOULD) open a welcome center for our school district similar to those you find along the highway when you enter a new state. I love those places. They are great. I like to stop whether I need to use the restroom or not – though at my age I usually do!

The staff at these centers is always helpful. They provide maps and brochures and tell you which roads to take and which ones are undergoing construction. They offer advice about hotels and restaurants. What's not to love?

We need a similar center for our district, I stated. Who is helping all these newcomers? Yes, we are growing by over 5,000 students, but we are probably losing a couple thousand and replacing them - plus our high school seniors are graduating and being replaced by kindergartners. All told, we will probably open school next year with over 20,000 students who are new to our district. Just who is helping their parents navigate such an immense organization like ours?

My friend just chuckled and repeated the words of the legendary Buddy Holly, *"That'll be the day."*

Not too long after that, one of the Superintendent's top aides was in my office about a separate issue. Somewhere in the conversation I mentioned my idea. Once again, I prefaced it with SOMEBODY SHOULD.

To my surprise, she nearly jumped out of her boots (a shout out to all our readers in Texas) and exclaimed the Superintendent had the same idea. In fact, he had already created and received Board approval for a new position. It laid dormant but available for the right person. She was so excited, and I was so surprised – and frightened.

As you can guess, we began having regular meetings. In fact, in an effort to build support, she would arrange meetings with various assistant superintendents, and I would have to go in and present my idea and try to convince them of the many ways it would benefit their respective departments. Some were more receptive than others, but in the end she brought the question full circle – or maybe it was more of a statement: **"You are planning to be our new Customer Service Administrator, aren't you?"**

Gulp. Double gulp. This was not my plan. Let me repeat…SOMEBODY SHOULD…not me. I was actually brought on with the understanding I would one day move into the leadership role of our Office of Student Assignment and then on to become a superintendent. I was pursuing my doctorate in Educational Leadership at the University of North Carolina. To take it further, since we had no professional organization for student assignment folks, I established one and was quickly gaining a reputation as a leader in my field. With all this going on, there was no thought of changing course and becoming the customer service guy!

She pressed me for an answer, and, as you can deduce, I decided to try it. I figured it would be a short term detour. After all, when would I ever get another opportunity to create a department from scratch? That just doesn't happen in the world of school system administration. I was given the keys to the kingdom. We reconstructed the first floor of our central office building (which was purchased long ago from IBM and contains a very interesting layout). I began my new job in February with a target date for opening on June 7, 2000. Those few months leading up to the opening were used for planning, information gathering, ordering supplies and various other tasks that I never saw coming.

Personnel

Staffing was tricky. One of our challenges was to staff the new center without any additional personnel. Hmmm.

Fortunately, it worked out great. The Public Information Office and the Office of Student Assignment donated one receptionist each with the attached expectation that the new Welcome Center will greatly reduce the number of customer contacts by handling many of the incoming telephone, face-to-face and e-mail inquiries. In fact, the position donated by the Office of Student Assignment was actually funded by our English as a Second Language (ESL) Department and is still operating under the same agreement. It's a pretty sweet arrangement. The employee reports to me, but anytime she needs office supplies, I send her to see her sugar daddy in the ESL department – you know, the guy with access to the federal funding!

Another position was gained by taking in the icon mentioned earlier. You remember, our building's front desk receptionist who started this whole mess by sending me all those unrelated calls. Since all of her customers would be coming through the new Center, she needed to be a part of it. And we were sure thankful for her expertise. Interestingly, we asked our phone service provider to run a study in order to find out just how many calls were coming in to our district's main number. We were astounded at how many more calls were coming in than could be handled by a single operator. We can only imagine how many frustrated callers were not able to get through prior to the opening of the center!

The final piece of the puzzle was one I am still scratching my head over. The superintendent's aide, who was overseeing this whole transition, "convinced" me it would be a good idea to supervise the building's mailroom. Even though it had nothing to do with the mission of the new Welcome Center, it came with a person who could finish her work in about four hours each day and, thereby, give me four hours of availability to assist with customer service duties. While it sounded like a good idea at the time, what I soon found out was that anytime the mailroom clerk had to be away from the office, one of my other customer service representatives (or moi) would have to fill in, thus leaving us really short handed.

Oh well. You live and learn – even from mistakes. I take heart in Bon Jovi's profound lyric, *"You can't win until you're not afraid to lose."*

Today

Consider yourself officially invited to come and visit our Welcome Center next time you are in Raleigh. We are open weekdays from 8:00 am until 5:00 pm. When you enter our central office building you will be greeted by a friendly security guard who will assist you with signing in and obtaining your visitor badge. She will ask who you are visiting. Tell her you want to go to the Welcome Center. She'll point the way. We are about 30 feet to her left.

When you come through the door you may notice a distant beeping sound. That is my fancy schmancy doorbell indicating I have a visitor. It also keeps a running tally of guests. To your right is a comfortable waiting area with seating for eight. Straight ahead is an L-shaped counter with a computer/phone station. I always have a representative stationed at the counter to greet and assist you. There is also a table and chairs for anyone that wants to complete a job application or any other task requiring a work area. There is a working kiosk which provides Internet access to guests. It is often used for job seekers, folks checking e-mail while waiting for a meeting, and parents needing to complete the system's online volunteer application. However, even cooler, is the kids' kiosk that was donated by IBM shortly after we opened. It is a colorful and stimulating piece of furniture that included a built in computer loaded with intriguing children's games. Frequently, I watch parents finish their business and try to leave only to hear the protests of their kids for just a little more time.

In addition to the furniture, there are multiple information sources located in the Welcome Center. Magazine racks are loaded with brochures, flyers and basically anything I can get my hands on that might be of interest to visitors.

If you come to visit, make sure I take you on the tour. In addition to the Welcome Center, I would take you to the office of the aforementioned ESL liaison. Because she helps people from all over the world, her customers are often so thankful they return to bring her a gift from their homeland. We proudly refer to her office as the museum. Other employees from our building like to come by periodically to check out any new "exhibits" she may have added. It is quite a collection of pictures, knick-knacks and the like.

I would also take you to the call center. Essentially, this is a large office in the back hall that houses three call stations. Since we rotate our team responsibilities, when not serving at the counter in the Welcome Center, you can often find us in the call center assisting callers and answering e-mail that arrives via the district website.

If, through reading this chapter, you start getting thoughts about designing a Welcome Center for your school or district, call me. I would love to discuss the possibilities and ask you the tough questions that will need to be addressed before proceeding. Research and planning, along with a clear set of expectations, will go a long way toward creating a successful center. I would be privileged to cheer you on as you make your way through the process.

Do what you know how to do well

And that's be you

<u>Whistling In The Dark</u> – They Might Be Giants

Customer Service Revival

We're gonna rock this town / Rock it inside out
We're gonna rock this town / Make 'em scream and shout
Let's rock, rock, rock, man, rock / We're gonna rock 'til we pop
Gonna roll 'til we drop / Rock this town / Rock it inside out

<u>Rock This Town</u> – Stray Cats

> *Next phase, new wave, dance craze, anyways*
> *It's still rock and roll to me*
> <u>Still Rock and Roll</u> – Billy Joel

So, after tolerating all these pages of far-out stories and suggestions, you think your school or district is ready for a customer service revival? Great! The time has arrived. What a wonderful way to send a message to the fine folks of your community – a message that you care about them and appreciate their support. Let me share a few thoughts to get you moving in the right direction – and do whatever you can to get your principal or superintendent to read this chapter (if not already engrossed in the fine literature that was the all the other chapters).

Leadership

> *Come gather 'round people wherever you roam*
> *And admit the waters around you have grown*
> <u>The Times They Are A' Changin'</u> – Bob Dylan

There is a really smart commercial on TV right now, "If Roadies Ran the World." It's a great look at what real communication and organization can do. However humorous the spot may be, reality states that **customer service revival is not a grass-roots movement. It starts at the top.** Unfortunately, I have met many school/district leaders that don't seem to think it is worthy of their time. After all, they have more important things to do than to offer an olive branch to the local taxpayers (sarcasm, in case you missed it).

Yes, I recognize it is entirely possible for a group of underlings to ignite a revival. But without the approval, check that, without the **participation** of the leader, chances for failure and burnout are high and chances for long-term success are slim.

I especially think NEW leaders should consider undertaking a full-fledged customer service revival. Why? First of all, new leaders make promises about responding to the needs of the community, involving parents as decision-makers. They have no choice but to issue such commitments. It is the politically correct stance. And let's face it, including your community is a great idea and will pay sustaining dividends if done properly.

Couple those promises with the new leader's need for putting his own stamp on the institution, and you have a wonderful recipe for customer service revival. You see, **new leaders need to come in with a plan, and they need to make a visible change very early in their reign** – preferably within the first 90 days. Some might say this is the period before the honeymoon ends, however the honeymoon may end sooner than later if the new change ruffles too many (or the wrong) feathers.

Customer service revival is a great plan because it allows the new leader to bring about a change that typically causes a paradigm shift and some new ways of doing business, but without getting existing employees too disgruntled. It is something the community will readily support and even the grumpy employees won't be able to complain – at least not publicly. Customer service upgrades can usually be implemented rather quickly and are relatively pain-free.

In order for the leader to initiate a revival, he must demonstrate two very important character traits: courage and humility. First, the leader must have the courage to issue a "thou shalt" mandate outlining the specific expectations and procedures that **will** be followed by all staff. Secondly, the leader must never think himself above those expectations and procedures. To the contrary, he must be first in line to demonstrate the level of humility needed for genuine customer-first interactions. The higher up the food chain we go, the more difficult this becomes.

A leader willing to set the example and then hold others accountable to that example will find customer service revival both rewarding and refreshing.

Audit

Okay, so you have a leader with the courage and humility to move forward with your customer service revival. What first?

That's simple. First, we measure the current level of service being offered throughout the district. How do you measure customer service? Good question. Obviously (or maybe not so obviously), undercover customer contacts will need to take place and numerical scores issued. I admit it is a form of secret shopping, but on steroids. It starts with the same concept but takes it to a whole new level if done properly. Below are a few tips regarding the five W's.

Don't Hire the House Band

1. **WHO** – To start with, don't try to do this yourself. While everyone fancies himself a perfect candidate to be a secret shopper, hire a professional. Better to bring in a consultant and later on think you could have done it yourself than to announce your intentions, get halfway into the project and then wish you would have heeded my advice. I've seen it done right, and I've seen it done wrong. It has the potential to be ugly if done haphazardly. And consider this, if the audit, which is a document of public record and one I am quite certain a local reporter would be interested in reading, comes back exposing a lot of dirty laundry, you would rather have the out-of-towner be the bearer of bad news than anyone living inside the district boundaries. Trust me on this one. And regarding your consultant, find one that only works with school customer service. Don't bring in one that specializes in restaurants, hospitals or other corporate venues. There is an enormous difference between corporate customer service and agency customer service. Besides the profit versus non-profit bottom line variation, there is also the respect factor. You see, grading the current performance is only half the task of a quality audit. The other half is the recommendations for improvement. Without them, the audit will serve only to stir up trouble and leave you with the same problem you wanted to fix, only with public attention brought to it. The recommendations need to be both strategic and reasonable. Does that mean bringing in some clown to write up a report listing a need for the three mores (more staff, more funding, more training)?

    Nope. That would be the easy way out. Your consultant should be reputable and one whose recommendations will have meat. In short, one who has worked in a school at some point in life. You know as well as I do, school people are the worst for wanting to make sure their trainers and consultants have "been in the trenches." If you have never stood in front of a class full of students for 180 school days, they don't care too much for your advice. Keep that in mind when hiring your auditor.

No Impromptu Jam Sessions

2. **WHAT** – Be sure your consultant is planning to utilize a pre-determined, standardized grading rubric for scoring your personnel. Remove as much subjectivity as possible. Many of the tips listed in previous chapters of this book can be part of your rubric. Look over the rubric prior to beginning the audit and customize the standards for your district. Be sure your audit includes numerical scores for site visits and phone calls as well as a grade for the website – after all, it has quickly become the single most important customer service tool and should only increase in importance in the coming years. I would also suggest your audit include a look at how e-mail messages are responded to by principals and central office administrators. I typically don't give numerical scores to e-mail, but I do look for trends and offer observations based on my findings. Every audit should also include an executive summary.

Planning the Tour

3. **WHERE** – Before you commission the audit, you will need to decide which sites you want measured. This is typically a very easy decision for a small school district. You probably want every school and your administration building visited. However, if you work in a larger district, it can become a little more complicated. For instance, my district has many administrative buildings. Not all deal with the general public. Perhaps they wouldn't need site visits, but would do a lot of business by phone or e-mail. Or perhaps I really want to focus on certain "public access" departments more than others. In many districts the offices of human resources, student assignment and special education deal with public interaction extensively. But the offices of foreign language instruction, staff development and accounting may not. Or, since the price of your audit will likely be based on the number of sites being tested, some districts may want to

audit just their magnet schools, or just their elementary schools, or some other subset of schools. Regardless of the reasons, it is good to have an idea of where your consultants will go prior to making the initial call for their services.

"According to a spokesperson for the band…"

4. **WHEN** – The important "when" question is this: When do you announce that you have contracted for a customer service audit? The date of your announcement is more important than you might think. Some prefer to announce right away. While this is certainly a straightforward approach, and successfully eliminates any excuses from school or central office administrators about "being set up", it also provides opportunity for skewed audit responses. Obviously, if they know your undercover consultant is coming, they will clean up the house – only to return to reality when he leaves town. On the other hand, not announcing until after the measurement has already occurred can result in hostile school and central office staff who feel as if they have been given an overdose of "gotcha!" And in unionized districts, especially, that can get ugly.

So when is the best time? You really need to analyze your situation. In most cases, I recommend making an early announcement but without specifics. Since customer service audits done correctly are often very lengthy reports (an audit for a district with ten schools will probably contain close to 200 pages) and take a lot of time to assemble, I suggest announcing the commission of the audit right after signing the contract – but without specific dates. Tell them auditors will be calling, visiting and writing "sometime this Fall." That let's them know it is happening without watering down the results. Of course, if they want to put on a dog and pony show for every customer over the next six months because they think it could be an auditor, then you have really accomplished something. Keep up the good work.

The Agent's Spin

5. **WHY** – Please be ready to tell people why you want this audit before your consultant gets to town. Beyond just the reasons,

consider the way you will tell them. You probably don't want to step on toes and hurt feelings, at least not until the report comes back. In addition to your staff, be ready to explain to your Board of Education and your local media why this is going to be a healthy exercise for your school district. Be prepared to comment on your commitment to excellence and your desire for "kaisen", or continuous improvement (impressed by my command of the Japanese language?). Perhaps even have your Public Information Officer draft a press release and put a notice on your website explaining the benefits of a customer service audit. Ask yourself, "How would Wolfman Jack say it?"

Can you tell I am passionate about the auditing process? I have conducted many of them. They are a lot of work, but the findings and recommendations can lead to sweeping changes that send a loud and clear message to your parents and the entire community. If you haven't been through one, please consider it. Just knowing your school or district is being measured can be of great benefit.

Standardize

There is no way to tell if you have a Number 1 hit on the Billboard charts without a system of standardization – or unless you are tight with Dick Clark. It's done the same way each week. So too, we need to set up a way to communicate our expectations. After you have measured your current level of service, it is time to establish a set of guiding principles for ALL employees and volunteers to follow. The hardest part about this task is getting started. So much to do, how do we get our heads around it? I suggest biting off small chunks. Draft a table of contents and then start filling it in.

Perhaps you can use the three genres of service mentioned earlier in the book as a starting point. Decide what the expectations are going to be when dealing with visitors, callers and e-mail. Get these expectations in writing and get them in the hands of every employee and volunteer in the district. Once you start the brainstorming process, ideas will flow and a helpful manual will ensue. The biggest problem may be deciding the breadth, or scope, of the document. I have crafted customer service standards manuals for many districts and they typically run 30 or 40 pages in length.

Once you have decided on the standards that will receive the "thou shalt" knighting, then you need to choose your method(s) for delivering the manual to the masses. I understand it may not be a welcomed mandate. The key will be to emphasize how this standards manual is going to help us serve our customers better. It is hard to argue with that goal. Try telling them this:

> "In an effort to offer the best possible service to our community, we are going to implement the customer service standards included in this manual. They will become the 'mode of operations' followed by all staff and volunteers."

OR

> "You may be doing a great job serving your customers. But, I'll bet all of us, at one time or another, have had to play the recovery game when a co-worker did not treat a customer properly and, consequently, the customer's anger was taken out on you! If we all follow these written principles, then you should never have to recover again."

Will it come directly from the superintendent to the principals? Should it be an e-mail memo to all employees with a link to a new customer service portal on the intranet site? Should it be a follow up document handed out at a district-wide customer service seminar? There are many ways to skin this cat, and one size definitely does not fit all. You will have to consider the culture of your district personnel and make the best choice for your folks. The only wrong way I can think of, and to my knowledge it did happen in a megadistrict recently with horrendous fallout, is to not tell your employees anything and let them find out from the media. Totally not cool!

Train

How do you get into the Rock 'n Roll Hall of Fame? Practice, practice, practice. Or in the case of customer service: train, train train. As mentioned in the No Soup For You chapter, the need for customer service training exists in every school and district. Unfortunately, very few are doing much about it. If you are serious about customer service revival, then **establish a training plan that includes both existing employees (at all levels!) and employees that will be hired in the coming months and years**. Be sure the training is fun. It should be conducted by someone with a passion for the topic. Please don't assign the duty to someone on staff who will merely see it as another unwanted item on the stressed out to-do list. Who is your very best customer service agent? Maybe that person could teach the rest of us. If nobody comes to mind as a stellar candidate for leading the training, then pony up the cash to hire someone from outside to do it. Not only will it be a treat for your staff to learn from the expert, it also sends a loud and clear message about the importance of the topic. Like I tell my kids, I am spending a lot of money on your piano lessons, I need to hear more than just "Mary Had A Little Lamb"!

Recognize

If I leave here tomorrow / Would you still remember me?
Free Bird – Lynyrd Skynyrd

What are you doing to recognize the people in your district who are truly serving customers in an exemplary fashion? Consider strategies to publicly thank them for their efforts – while simultaneously showcasing their skills in a way that sets a great example for peers.

From a district perspective, **consider honoring schools that serve their customers well**. I am a huge fan of a program that has been taking place in South Carolina for years. It is called the "Red Carpet Schools" program. There, the state's Department of Education organizes an award for which individual schools can apply and win. A principal completes an application and, if they get through the initial screening, an undercover consultant will "shop" the school and provide a grade. The schools with the high grades are awarded the inscribed red carpets. Having a red carpet hanging in a school entranceway is quite an honor in South Carolina. I remember one district in which every school but one had been awarded a red carpet over the years. You can imagine the pressure on that last school to make the needed changes and win the award.

It would be wonderful if your state department of education would be willing to organize a program similar to South Carolina's Red Carpet Schools. However, if you are in a larger district, say with 30 or more schools, you could initiate one yourself. While it is similar to the aforementioned customer service audit, a recognition program should probably be a follow up to a customer service audit. I suggest conducting a new customer service audit every 18-24 months. However, if your district has had a couple audits in recent years, then I would recommend considering a recognition program.

Positive Deviance

Perhaps you are familiar with a popular book entitled <u>Influencer</u>, written by Patterson, et al. (the same authors wrote <u>Crucial Conversations</u>). This book makes frequent reference to the concept of "positive deviance". I believe it is very applicable to any school or district wanting to engage in customer service revival.

You see, as educators, we typically look for the kid in class who is cutting up or somehow distracting the class. We single out that student because he is negatively deviating from our rules or expectations, and we then attempt corrective measures.

Similar but different (?), we can think of positive deviance as a three-step process. First, we select a problem – a behavior exhibited by a lot of employees and, in our opinion, in need of correction. Then we study the settings where the problem should flourish but doesn't. Last, we identify the unique habits of those who succeed despite the conditions. Once we have identified those unique habits, we can methodically turn the ship around.

Let's apply positive deviance to a real-life customer service problem. Say we want everyone in our school district to answer the phone with a proper four-part greeting as discussed in an earlier chapter. We'll assume few people are currently doing it and, in fact, most people are using only a one- or two-part greeting. So, instead of singling out the employees **not** using the four-part greeting, we actually find the few who, though not expected to, **are** implementing the four-part greeting. We'll observe the behaviors unique to this subgroup and see if there is anything we can replicate through our training program.

The larger your employee-base, the more you may want to consider a positive deviance approach.

It's not too late
To turn this ship around
It's Not Too Late - The Monkeys

The Secret To Great Service

Don't accept average habits
Open your heart and push the limits

<u>Push The Limits</u> - Enigma

Sometimes we learn great lessons from tragic stories. In fact, in a weird way I suppose that is a tragedy in itself that it takes a serious wake-up call just to get our attention. But we are a fast-paced generation, and that's just how we roll.

I received such a wake-up call a few years ago. You see, early one morning when Lori and I were getting ready for work, we had the morning news on and saw a story about a police officer who had been shot in the line of duty. It was a routine traffic stop during the middle of the night. I imagine it started out similar to a hundred he had done prior. But this time the person he pulled over shot him in the face.

Lori and I were stunned. You see this police officer was a neighbor of ours, and more than that, his wife was my little girl's teacher. As you can imagine, the officer frequently visited the classroom, and the kids would climb all over him on the playground. They loved him and, deservedly, he was their hero. So how do I tell my 6-year-old that her hero had just been shot during the night, and he is in the hospital clinging for his life?

I took the kids to school that day, and I remember how eerily quiet the halls were as they lacked the usual morning perkiness for which the school was known. It was an environment I never want to experience again.

While this unfortunate event occurred during the middle of the week, allow me to fast forward a couple days to the next weekend. I finished stomping around the yard coughing and sneezing and exhibiting my weekly tantrum (I just love cutting grass), when it occurred to me I should drive over to my neighbor's house to see if his yard needed mowing.

To be honest, I was really hoping his yard did not need any of my time. I figured, and yes I realize I am a worm, it was the thought that counts and the fact I drove over there with my lawn mower was good enough to make me feel righteous even if I didn't actually cut grass. After all, I am an important person with lots of important things to do. Screwed up – I know.

Well, I arrived at the house and, sure enough, it needed mowing. It felt like I was smack in the middle of a scary movie. Both cars were in the driveway, and I noticed all the signs of a normal household – the grill, the swing set, etc. However, there was pollen all over cars, and I could tell they haven't been moved in days. The family was apparently living at the hospital.

I fired up the lawn mower and began cutting the grass. Interestingly, after about ten minutes, I was overcome by a genuine sense of humility – obviously something quite lacking in my life. After twenty minutes I was walking around behind my push mower with a silly grin on my face. I wanted to do more for my friend. I wanted to clean his gutters or trim his hedges. However, I am not skilled in the area of household maintenance, and I'm sure he wouldn't want me messing with his stuff.

What I learned that day is a lesson in servanthood. I humbled myself, took on an unpleasant task and did it for the benefit of someone else. I was not going to get paid, be awarded a medal or even receive a thank you. In fact, to this day, I don't think the family ever knew I cut their grass one Saturday several years ago.

But I remember it vividly. It was a lesson long overdue. For once in my life, I put my own wants/needs aside and sacrificed for the sake of another. I spent my time, my energy and any resource I had available for my neighbor.

This hard lesson is applicable in distinguishing the difference between *good* customer service and *great* customer service. You see, **good customer service is all about what you do**. If you do the things listed in this book, such as standing to greet visitors and ending conversations by inviting further interaction, then you will be good at customer service. I think I offer good customer service based on the *things I do*.

However, as I have learned in recent years, **great customer service is not based on what you do, but rather on who you are!** It is founded on the character you possess and how you reveal it when relating to others. If you possess solid character, rest assured it will bubble up to the surface. Great customer service requires that same sense of humility I experienced cutting my neighbor's grass. There have been a few times when I have set aside my pride and humbly served with the same level of submission and sacrifice – expending my time, energy, knowledge and any other resource I could muster – for the sake of a customer.

And I'm here to tell you, offering great customer service is very satisfying. But I would be lying if I said I treat all my customers that way. I don't. It is my goal – but I have a long way to go.

To add a Rock 'n Roll perspective, Elvis recorded more than 900 songs, but only 17 were Number 1 hits. The Beatles, arguably the most influential band in rock history, made more than 200 songs with only

10% paying off as number ones. Heck, the Rolling Stones are still at it and have achieved only eight. Surely, there is still hope for me.

> *Don't stop thinking about tomorrow*
> <u>Don't Stop</u> – Fleetwood Mac

Maybe you live on that mountaintop of great service. Maybe you give all you have for the sake of the customer in every encounter. If so, enjoy the good feelings that accompany your authentic humility. Currently, I only have a time-share there, but I hope to join you one day as a permanent resident. I have scratched my way to the top of the mountain a few times and peeked out over the horizon…it is a beautiful place and filled with beautiful people.

We started this book with a pop quiz. If you are like most people, then you believe you are currently offering good service. If so, then strive for great service. But for the many we have identified as not currently offering good service, then tell them about the suggestions that will at least get them to the level of good. It is hard to change who they are, but you can certainly influence what they do.

And the best news is my friend and hero recovered nicely, returned to the police department and has since welcomed another child to the family. How's that for a happy ending?

Customer service is not something to check off the to-do list. It is an ongoing challenge that reveals more about yourself than you ever before imagined. Enjoy the journey. **Rock on!**

> *What a long, strange trip it's been*
> <u>Truckin'</u> – The Grateful Dead

For a customer service audit, standards handbook, consulting or training (or any other reason), feel free to contact Jeff Nash at janash@turningpointsolutions.biz or by phone at 919-412-7947.

Thank you for reading.

Made in the USA